the strateg

How to maximise value on the sale or transition of your business

Martin Checketts

Published in Australia by Abington Park Media

First published in Australia 2010

Checketts, Martin
THE STRATEGIC EXIT – how to maximise value on the sale or transition of your business

ISBN: 978-0-9807579-0-3

Cover layout and design by Kate Forehan, KFD
Typesetting by TDAdesign.com.au
Edited by Melita Granger and Jo Tayler
Printed by Australian Book Connection

Disclaimer

All care has been taken in the preparation of the information in this work, but no responsibility can be accepted by the publisher or author for any damages resulting from the misinterpretation of this work. All contact details given in this book were current at the time of publication, but are subject to change.

The advice given in this book is based on the experience of individuals, is general in nature, and does not take into account the particular circumstances of any person. Professionals should be consulted for specific advice on individual problems. To the maximum extent permissible by law, the author and publisher shall not be responsible to any person with regard to any loss or damage caused directly or indirectly by the information in this book.

Foreword

Having sold a business after 25 years of operation, I know the importance of good advice.

While there have been many books and articles written about exit options available to business owners, this book summarises all the options in an easy-to-read and easy-to-understand fashion.

As Martin explains, an exit is not something you think about just before you want to sell your business. Implementing Martin's strategies to increase the value of your business will help you maintain a professional, productive and profitable business during the period of your ownership. Then at the time of sale, preparation won't be so all-encompassing that your business will experience disruption.

Understanding the options is the starting point, and this book does that very well. In my view, it is clear, concise and accurate.

The Strategic Exit is a must read for owners of SME businesses.

Paul Veith, Founder of IPA Personnel

About the Author

Martin Checketts is a well-known expert on the sale and transition of private and family-owned businesses.

Martin advises clients on preparing their businesses for sale, staged successions, mergers and acquisitions, shareholders agreements, capital raisings, and other aspects of corporate and commercial law. He is a qualified lawyer in England, Wales and Australia and is a partner with Mills Oakley Lawyers.

Martin lives in Melbourne with his wife and three children. In his spare time he enjoys spending time with his family, rock music and supporting causes related to autism and intellectual disability.

mchecketts@millsoakley.com.au

www.millsoakley.com.au
www.thestrategicexit.com

Contents

Preface

My interest in owner-managed business was sparked at an early age.

For many generations, various branches of the Checketts family have owned butcher's shops in the south and west midlands of England. Some of those businesses are still thriving today – such as Checketts of Ombersley, a fourth-generation family business that was established by my great-great uncle Thomas Green Checketts in 1902.

My grandfather Jack was a master butcher who spent most of his waking hours at the shop. Indeed, rumour has it he sometimes slept there!

One of my earliest memories is of visiting my grandfather at work. I distinctly remember that pristine little shop, which offered only the best cuts of meat and the finest homemade sausages and pies. My grandfather's pride as a hard-working business owner shone through like a beacon and reflected back on me and the whole family.

My grandfather was comfortably well-off for most of his adult life. However, a number of bad investments meant that in his later years he had few assets other than the business. But when he finally retired, did he sell the business and live happily ever after? No. He simply shut the door and walked away. After a lifetime of hard work, he had little to show for it.

Fast forward a few years and it was my father John's turn to become the entrepreneur of the family.

Originally a talented school teacher, my father always had a passion for business. In his mid-thirties he left the education world to set up a life insurance brokerage, after a short stint with a merchant bank. With no business contacts at all, he started out by simply walking up and down residential streets, knocking on doors and introducing himself to prospective clients. From those humble beginnings he grew a large and profitable financial planning business in the pioneering days of what was then, in the early 1980s, an embryonic profession.

My teenage years and early twenties were spent around my father's business; again I shared his pride and sense of purpose in the successful enterprise that he had created. However, the golden period didn't last long. With responsibility came stress and my father started to suffer from migraines. By the age of 53 he was unable to continue working. He sold his share in the business to his co-owner and retired.

My father had learned from my grandfather's mistakes. During the good years he had taken his own prudent financial advice and put away significant sums of money in safe investments. He also had the foresight to purchase a generous income protection policy.

Of course, my father also received the sale proceeds from his share of the business.

The business was by that time a valuable asset which was well managed and underwritten by solid renewal commissions and other recurring revenue streams. My father was also protected by a shareholders agreement, which gave him the right to sell to his co-owner for a fair price, even though poor health meant that he was effectively a 'forced seller'.

My father's achievements in my formative years profoundly influenced my career choice as a corporate lawyer and my perspective on wealth creation, business, and life in general.

This book is permeated with my father's lessons, and is dedicated to him.

Acknowledgments

This book draws on the experience and sound advice of so many people with whom I have worked over the years – my valued clients, other professional advisers, and my colleagues at Mills Oakley. There are unfortunately far too many of you to name individually.

Working with all of you has taught me so much about the subject-matter of this book. As such, this book is largely a compilation of collective knowledge rather than my own unique theory or view of the world. For this, I thank you all.

I would also like to thank and acknowledge the following particular people:

Julie Postance – for your wisdom, encouragement and support from the beginning of the process. You challenged my thinking at every stage, and helped me to create a product which is greatly superior (and less legalistic!) than my original efforts. Your input was invaluable.

Alan Rodway – our Ownership Monster seminars were the genus of various chapters of this book. In the world of business succession, you taught me that the 'soft' or emotional issues are actually often the hardest ones to deal with.

Anthony Dobbyn and Anthony Carafa – an inspirational breakfast meeting with you helped me enormously to structure the chapters and key messages of this book.

Melita Granger and Jo Tayler – for your skill, attention to detail and frankness as editors.

Simon Kneebone – for highlighting the key themes through your fantastic illustrations. It was a pleasure to work with you.

Mark Stephen – for introducing me to the 'mirror test'.

For reviewing and appraising parts of the early manuscript: Tony Beck, Anthony Carafa, Mark Carrazzo, Jo Checketts, John Checketts, Bernadette Cottom, Brandon Craven, Anthony Dobbyn, Mark Emerson, Dallas Ibrhaim, Anthony Lane, John Nerurker, Toby Norgate, Peter Piasente, Hayley Preston, Warren Scott, Jeremy Steele, Rose Uren, Andrew Walker, Vaughan Webber and Xavier West. Your comments and insights helped me to create a much better and sharper product. Any remaining errors are, of course, entirely my own.

Last, but by no means least, my family – Laurie, Madeleine, Noah and Isaac. Your ongoing love and support is everything to me. Thank you for tolerating me juggling a full-time job and writing this book. Without you, it would not have happened.

About this book

If you act strategically, growing and selling your business will be the biggest and most financially rewarding achievement of your working life. It will also provide you with the freedom to follow your dreams and achieve your other life goals.

It is such a shame that so many hard working business owners don't achieve this because they lack the foresight, skills or knowledge.

In this book, I will share with you the strategies that I have learned through advising business owners in a variety of industries over many years.

You will learn how to:

- grow and capture value in your business and translate this into significant capital appreciation on sale

- address the emotional, personal and non-financial issues that may accompany your business succession process

- plan for and implement your exit strategy, including:
  - deciding which strategy is right for you
  - beating procrastination (the 'too busy' syndrome)
  - selecting and managing your professional advisory team
  - learning effective negotiation skills.

The strategies in this book are not just theories. They have been tried and tested many times in the real world.

Through employing these strategies, I have seen many business owners realise significant wealth. Some do this just once and then move on to other interests. Others become serial entrepreneurs, buying, growing and selling businesses time and time again.

Succession stories

Throughout this book you will find 'succession stories' and other brief, fictional case studies that highlight real-life issues. The characters and scenarios are not based on any particular person or business. Any similarity is entirely coincidental.

Terminology

For simplicity and ease of reading, I have generally used the word 'business' instead of terms that describe the legal structure through which the business is operated (e.g. a company, partnership or trust).

When I refer to a 'business sale', in reality that transaction may take a number of different forms (e.g. a sale of the entire issued share capital of a company, a sale of assets or a share buy-back or capital return). There are many important differences between these sale structures, but an in-depth analysis is outside the scope of this book.

This book has its limitations!

As you will appreciate, this book is not a substitute for legal, financial, taxation or other professional advice. You should always seek individual professional advice in connection with your exit strategy. Indeed, as you will read later in this book, working with the right professional team is one of the critical aspects of ensuring that your transaction is successful.

Let's get down to business

I do hope that you get a lot out of this book.

Once you have read and absorbed it, I would love to hear your feedback and your own succession story. Please e-mail me at mchecketts@millsoakley.com.au or visit www.thestrategicexit.com.

ARE YOU AND YOUR BUSINESS 'SUCCESSION READY'? TAKE THIS QUICK TEST!

1   **Have you written down your financial, business and other life goals?** Or are all your waking hours absorbed by the day-to-day running of your business with little planning for the future?

2   **Have you assessed your personal financial position and whether your assets and retirement savings are sufficient to achieve those goals?** Or are you in the dark as to how much it will cost to fund the goals and lifestyle you aspire to?

3   **Have you discussed your goals with your spouse or business partner(s)?** Or do you just expect that they will fall into line with your plans?

4   **Have you documented the strategy for your business and the responsibilities of key stakeholders in order to achieve that strategy?** Or is this just in your head?

5   **Have you factored known or unknown health issues into your plans?** Or are you simply crossing your fingers that you will be fit and able to work as you have always done?

6   **Are systems and procedures in place to ensure that the business could run smoothly in your absence?** Or does the business rely heavily on your day-to-day input?

7   **Do you have robust financial reporting systems in place?** Or is the financial information in relation to your business incomplete, unreliable or difficult to decipher?

8   **Is there a clear separation between your business and personal assets and liabilities?** Or are these intermingled?

9   **Are your senior employees appropriately motivated and remunerated and bound by restraint-of-trade obligations?** Or are those people a 'flight risk' who could damage your business significantly if they decide to leave?

10 **Have you taken steps to protect your brand, logos and other intellectual property assets?** Or are you at risk of a competitor using these assets and jeopardising your brand or market position?

11 **Have you protected the revenue streams of your business through long-term contracts?** Or are those revenue streams based on one-off transactions, personal relationships or ad hoc arrangements?

12 **Is your corporate structure simple?** Or do you have a complex web of companies that would be difficult to understand and unravel?

13 **Are your IT systems appropriate and user-friendly?** Or do you rely heavily on manual record keeping or personalised IT solutions that are complex, outdated or difficult to understand?

14 **If you have business partners, is there a shareholders agreement or other document that contains clear mechanisms for selling or transitioning the business (or your equity interest)?** Or do you simply expect that these issues will be resolved when the time comes?

15 **Do you use professional advisers appropriately for the size and complexity of your business?** Or do you get by with minimum external help?

Chapter 1

The five key principles of business succession

In this chapter you will learn

the guiding principles for a successful exit strategy

The five key principles

There are two separate, yet complementary, aspects to my work as a corporate lawyer. The first involves advising business owners on their exit strategies. The second involves helping buyers to acquire businesses.

So, I have had the benefit of seeing business owners progress their exit strategies from 'both sides of the fence' – the sell side and the buy side.

When planning this book, I spent time reflecting on the many exit strategies that I have seen in my career. I looked to identify the factors that the most successful ones had in common, and then did the same for those that were less successful. I dusted off old files from transactions relating to businesses of all shapes and sizes, from small one-person operations to large multinational companies, and across many different industries.

Interestingly, it was often my work on the buy side, acting for large companies and private equity funds, that gave me the best insights into what can go right or wrong for the seller. These organisations are very sophisticated buyers of businesses. The ways in which they evaluate a business and negotiate the transaction provide so many valuable lessons about snares and pitfalls for the seller.

I also thought back on some of the tactics that I and other professional advisers have used over the years to get the best deal for our buyer clients. Some of those tactics were subtle or low-key, and others were aggressive or downright nasty! I then considered how sellers might best defend themselves against such tactics, avoid being ambushed, and stay in control throughout the process. From this analysis, the concept of 'the Strategic Exit' was born.

Unsurprising, the best sale outcomes that I have seen in my career were never a fluke. Five key principles stand out clearly to me as having underscored nearly all of them. These principles apply whether the business is large, small or somewhere in the middle, and irrespective of the industry sector in which the business operates.

The five key principles re-occur as important themes throughout this book. I have summarised them here at the beginning so that you can keep them in mind as you progress through the remaining chapters.

Key principle 1: A successful exit is planned.

A successful exit strategy is generally not achieved overnight. You should expect it to take months or years of preparation.

I have lost count of the number of business owners that I have seen jump quickly into a sale process without appropriate planning – either through lack of foresight or because an unexpected event (such as a health crisis) forces a quick sale.

Selling without proper preparation is like walking into the lion's den. The buyer, often with advice from people like me, will smell you coming from a mile away, tear your business apart piece by piece, and then watch as you either make reluctant concessions to get the deal done or run for the hills without a sale being concluded.

Instead, your succession planning process should begin *as early as possible.* This may seem a little paradoxical, but it should ideally begin *on the very first day that you buy or start the business.*

To plan a successful exit strategy, you need to apply what some people call the 'mirror test' to your business. This means that you must hold up a metaphorical mirror to the business and *critically appraise* what you see in all of its harsh reality, as if through the eyes of a prospective buyer. And as we all know, when looking in the mirror it can be hard to keep your objectivity!

The issues that are identified via the mirror test should then be addressed periodically, in manageable chunks, as an ongoing process of improvement in the months and years before your exit. There is little point in holding up the mirror for a 'warts and all' view of your business if you only do this just before you offer the business for sale. How will you ever get things fixed up in time?

Even if your exit won't occur for several years or decades, regularly taking time out to hold up the mirror in this way is also simply *good business practice.* It results in better processes, better management, less operational risk and increased profitability for your business. And all of these will be enjoyed by you in the short term whether you sell or not.

Key principle 2: Operate your business as a steward for the next owner.

Successful exits flow from an attitude of running your business not for immediate reward, but rather with a view to passing on something that is better, stronger and more secure to the next owner. This means that you will need to commit to a long term business strategy, and have the fortitude not to deviate from that strategy for short-term gain.

It also means that you must re-invest appropriately in the business and *not strip out every last dollar of profit along the way.* So, get used to living within your means.

While this may sound rather altruistic or 'noble', the concept that you should embrace is one of operating the business like a trustee or steward for your successor.

This approach will not only translate into real value in your pocket upon exit, but will also give you the satisfaction of leaving the legacy of a business that is strong enough to grow and thrive across generations.

Remember that the most successful transactions are the ones where the seller not only sells well, but also where the buyer *buys well.* If you sell a quality business, the buyer will not only pay you a good price for that business, but should also remain satisfied following the acquisition. Conversely, buyers who feel that they have been sold a 'dud' are highly motivated to hire a bulldog lawyer to scour back through the sale agreement and look for reasons to sue. And, believe me, they often find them!

Key principle 3: Reduce dependence on yourself.

Many business owners are surprised to hear that one of the biggest impediments to a successful exit strategy is *themselves.*

Generally speaking, private and family-owned businesses are extremely dependent on the contribution of their owner for their continued growth and success. This can create a major impediment for the buyer, who is then faced with the challenge of acquiring *your personal goodwill.*

Conversely, buyers will pay a premium for businesses that are not dependent on

5

the *personal goodwill* of the owner, but have their own *business goodwill* which will survive and flourish after the current owner has departed.

When this concept first dawned on one of my business owner clients, I remember him saying to me *'I don't have a business, I just have a job.'* He had realised that whilst his labours provided him with a good income from year to year, the business was so dependent on him that it was unsaleable.

Key principle 4: Timing is everything.

Selling your business at the right time is critical in ensuring maximum value.

If you are to sell your business for a substantial premium, you will need to do so when there is a favourable environment for your business, its industry sector and the economy in general. You need to sell when your business is *humming along* – profitable, vibrant, and with a good growth story.

Being able to sell at the right time means ensuring that:

- your business is always operated in a way that will make it attractive to prospective buyers. In this way, you can capitalise on any sale opportunities that arise unexpectedly
- you identify and build relationships with potential buyers of your business from an early stage
- your business, and you personally, are in a financial position that is strong enough that you (and not external factors) can dictate the time to sell.

It is alarming how many business owners I have seen enter into major commitments to buy their dream home or boat before they have sold (or even signed a contract to sell) their existing business. Commitments of this nature lead to major concessions being made in your sale process, to get the deal over the line at all costs.

I recall once working with a buyer client in negotiating a transaction where the seller let slip that he had already signed a contract to buy another business. Given the size of that other business, we strongly suspected that the seller needed the proceeds from this sale to complete on that other contract. You can imagine how we pushed that seller to the brink during those negotiations! The seller had sacrificed control over the timing of his exit, and paid dearly for it.

Key principle 5: Ensure that your business and life goals are clear and aligned.

A sale or other business transition is a significant happening in your life. You have usually been deeply invested in the business, both financially and emotionally, for many years – maybe even an entire lifetime.

If you have not spent time identifying and mapping out your business and life goals, it is unlikely that you will be able to figure out the right time to exit, either from a personal or a business perspective.

You may 'hang on' too long and risk damaging the business because your interests and passions lie elsewhere, or because you are no longer the right person to take the business to the next level.

Or you may leave too soon – perhaps without planning for the next stage of your life or giving thought to whether the sale proceeds will fund your lifestyle and future plans. In one extreme situation, I knew a business owner who regretted his decision to sell and retire early so much that he asked the buyer if he could come back and work in the business *for free!*

So, you should make sure that you regularly look ahead to assess, clarify and align your personal and business goals. Through doing this, you are more likely to make a better decision around the timing and strategy for your exit. You will also be better prepared to move on and enjoy the next stage of your life, whatever that may entail.

KEY LEARNINGS FROM THIS CHAPTER:

Remember the five key principles of business succession and apply them as you read the remainder of this book:

- A successful exit is planned

- Operate your business as a steward for the next owner

- Reduce dependence on yourself

- Timing is everything

- Ensure that your business and life goals are clear and aligned

Chapter 2

What is your business worth?

In this chapter you will learn

key valuation principles

and

how to apply valuation principles to maximise price on exit

Understanding valuation

I have heard countless people ask, *'What is my business worth?'*

The most trite (and perhaps the best) answer is *'As much as someone will pay for it.'*

In order to grow a business that will sell for the highest price, it is important that you understand the key principles of business valuation. You can then make changes to your business to increase its value in accordance with those principles.

Valuation methods

One of the first things most prospective buyers will do is engage an accountant to value your business.

The process of business valuation is sometimes described as a 'black art'. Whilst there is certainly a lot of science and rigour behind it, there is also an element of opinion and subjectivity.

When valuing your business, the accountant will look at your financial records and other relevant information and apply various methodologies, such as:

- *Multiple of earnings* – calculate the earnings of your business and apply a multiple to those earnings – for example, 4 x EBIT (earnings before interest and tax).
- *Discounted cash flow* – estimate future cash flow and discount it to give present values. Because this valuation methodology is forward-looking in nature, it is commonly used for start-up businesses or 'turnaround' situations (where the business has historically performed poorly, but significant improvement is expected in future).
- *Net asset value* – calculate the value of the assets of your business and then deduct the amount of its liabilities.
- *Industry 'rules of thumb'* – certain industries have historically applied valuation methodologies that are particular to those industries. For example, insurance brokerages are traditionally valued on a multiple of recurring revenue and real estate businesses are traditionally valued on a multiple of the rent roll earnings.

When valuing your business, the accountant will take into account more than one valuation methodology before coming to a final conclusion. For example, a multiple of EBIT may be calculated and then cross-checked against a net asset valuation.

When someone buys your business, what they are doing is converting an upfront capital sum (the purchase price) into an ongoing right to receive income (the profits of the business). When determining value a buyer will therefore generally be more interested in the profitability of your business than the value of its assets.

Accordingly, a multiple of earnings is usually the most favoured valuation method.

The multiple that is applied to the earnings of your business equates to the number of years over which the buyer should earn back their capital sum outlaid. For example, if the buyer is paying you a multiple of 3.5 x last year's EBIT, they are expecting to get their upfront capital back in 3.5 years (not taking into account any income tax to be paid on the profits of the business).

The size of the multiple reflects:

- the risk that the historical profits may not be sustained after your business has been bought and sold (the greater the risk, the lower the multiple); and
- the opportunity to increase the historical profits under the new ownership (the greater the opportunity, the higher the multiple).

Earnings taken into account for valuation

For the purpose of valuation, primary importance is placed on the earnings which were generated by your business in the last financial year. This highlights for you the key principle that timing is everything – your imperative must be to sell at a time when your business is good and profitable.

That said, just because your business did well last year, this does not necessarily mean that your sale price will be based solely on that year's earnings. The valuer may also take into account the earnings from prior years and/or projected future earnings.

For example, if your business has experienced a recent significant increase in earnings, there may be some concern about whether those earnings are sustainable in future. The valuer may therefore choose to average the earnings of your business over (say) the last three financial years.

The valuer may also apply different weightings to different years' earnings. For example, a higher percentage weighting may be applied to the earnings of your business in the current financial year, and a lower percentage weighting may be applied to the earnings in previous financial years.

Future earnings

Sellers often try to maximise their return by proposing a price which is based on a multiple of future projected earnings, i.e. the seller's prediction of how the business will perform after the buyer has bought it. And, no surprise, those projections invariably show a healthy future profit growth, for which the seller expects to be handsomely paid!

The reality is that without a compelling reason, it will be difficult for you to sell your business based on the *mere potential* to achieve future projected earnings. Or, if a buyer is to pay on that basis, an earn-out may be favoured. This is where part of the purchase price is deferred and paid later (e.g. after 18 months) depending on how the business performs in that period.

The relatively rare group of sellers who are able to convince a buyer that the earnings of their business will grow following the sale, and that the buyer should *pay upfront* for that growth, generally sell for a premium.

So, how can you join that elite group of sellers? The answer normally involves careful long-term planning. The 'text book' way in which I have seen it done is as follows:

- build a business model that is based on reliable recurring revenue streams (e.g. revenues from annual licensing fees, annual maintenance contracts, recurring retainer fees, or trail commissions)
- provide the potential buyer with 3+ years of rock solid historical financials, which:
  - are prepared by external accountants
  - show a sustainable growth trend in earnings
  - reflect performance which is substantially in accordance with detailed annual budgets
- give some legal comfort to the buyer that the growth trend is supportable, by ensuring that:
  - revenues are 'locked in' through long-term contracts which last for at least

the duration of the financial projections
- o expenses such as raw material and rental costs are similarly locked in
- o those long-term contracts do not have change of control clauses or prohibitions on assignment which would allow the customer or supplier to terminate upon a sale of the business
- o if the projected growth of the business is conditional upon the ability to acquire another particular business or asset, a legally-binding option or other right exists to ensure that business or asset can be acquired.

But hang on a moment, I hear you say. Get real! How many businesses are really built around the nirvana of recurring revenues and expenses that are locked in by solid long term contracts?

And I would agree with you. Most of the businesses that I advise do not fall into that category. It is also difficult to see how many of them could be substantially re-engineered to achieve this.

So, I acknowledge that the 'text book' approach will not work for everyone. That said, there is still one important part of this approach which every private and family business owner should adopt as part of their exit strategy. Even without the other parts, this factor alone may give you the biggest fighting chance of persuading a buyer to pay for your business based upon future financial projections.

So what is this special factor? *It is the disciplined preparation of detailed and accurate budgets in the years before you exit.*

Why is budgeting so powerful? The reason is that, at the most basic level, a financial projection is essentially nothing more or less than a *budget.* It is a forward-looking statement that predicts the revenues and expenditure of your business.

Put yourself in the sensible shoes of the buyer's accountants. If they are going to recommend a price for your business based on your future projections (or at least not actively try and dissuade the buyer from paying that price), they will need something concrete to back this up. What could be better than a track record of, say, three years where you have prepared a detailed annual budget and can demonstrate that the actual revenues and expenses of your business then closely mirrored what was budgeted? If your budgets were accurate historically, this gives *big comfort* that they will be accurate in future.

On the other hand, what if you have not prepared budgets in the years before the sale, but are now making bold financial projections in the hope of selling for an inflated price? You are serving up a reason for the buyer's accountants to attack your projections on a silver platter.

Similarly, if your previous budgets have proved to be wildly inaccurate, the buyer's accountants will also have plenty of ammunition to convince their client that they would be crazy to pay a price based on your projections. After all, your budgets have never translated into actual earnings before, so why should the buyer believe that things will be different this time? It takes a brave buyer to ignore the advice of their accountants when considering these issues, particularly if the buyer is a large company with detailed internal 'sign off' procedures.

Of course, adopting a robust and detailed budgeting process is also a great business discipline whether or not you sell. And if you do not have the skills to do this in-house, invest in some help from your accountant. *Remember – no budgets means little credibility for your financial projections.*

Common misconceptions about price and valuation

I sometimes see business owners disappointed with the amount that they receive on exit, not because they have necessarily done a bad deal, but because they did not have a strong grasp of a couple of key valuation concepts before they started the sale process.

One thing that is sometimes misunderstood by sellers is that only *maintainable* earnings are taken into account for the purpose of valuation.

This means that the valuer will adjust the earnings of your business downwards to take into account one-off or abnormal items. Here are some examples:

- Say you do not pay yourself, as an employee of the business, a decent salary. From a buyer's perspective, this means that the earnings of your business are artificially inflated, as the buyer would need to pay someone a market salary to do your job. The buyer will therefore take into account a market salary cost to reduce the earnings of your business before then applying a multiple to determine value.

- Say the earnings of your business last year included the sale of a one-off item or of a product line that has since been discontinued. The valuer would discount last year's earnings by the amount of those sales.

You should also bear in mind that the amount you will receive in your pocket upon sale is *generally less than the amount of the buyer's valuation.* Why is this? There are two main reasons:

- The amount of the net debts of your business will normally be deducted from the headline amount of the valuation. For example, say your business has annual EBIT of $1 million and bank debt of $500,000 (secured against the stock-in-trade). If a buyer pays you a price of 4 times EBIT, you will not receive $4 million in your pocket, as the bank will need to be paid out of the sale proceeds. Instead, you will receive only $3.5 million.

- You will only, of course, receive in your pocket the *after tax* return on your business sale. It is amazing how many business owners ignore the capital gains tax implications of the sale, and then get a nasty surprise when their tax return is prepared. The need for good tax advice in connection with your exit strategy is further discussed in chapter 10.

When thinking about selling your business, it is easy to be dazzled by the headline business valuation. However, you should always carefully consider and calculate how much you will actually receive in your pocket, so that you have realistic expectations.

Applying valuation principles to increase your sale price

Let's use a case study to examine how, using a basic understanding of valuation principles, you can make changes to increase the sale price of your business.

Paul's Cleaning Company

Four years ago Paul acquired a cleaning business, which he re-branded Paul's Cleaning Company. The business provides cleaning services to office premises. Paul is looking to retire and has put his business on the market to be sold.

When he bought the business, it had annual revenue of $20 million and annual profit of $3 million. Paul paid a multiple of three-times (3 x) profits, being $9 million.

So, applying basic valuation principles, there are only two ways in which Paul can increase the price of Paul's Cleaning Company above $9 million upon sale:

1 *increase the profits above $3 million* (either by growing revenue, reducing expenses or both) or

2 *increase the multiple upon sale* to greater than three times.

Increasing profits

Assume that when Paul sells the business he will sell at the same 3 x multiple of earnings at which he bought.

That being the case, it is a simple mathematical truth that for every $1 of additional earnings that Paul can create above $3 million, he will realise an additional $3 upon sale. This is the only time in Paul's business life when $1 will equal $3!

The effect of this multiplier is extremely potent. Just stop and think about it for a moment. *Every extra dollar of profit means an extra three dollars on sale.*

Truly appreciating the effect of this multiplier on your sale price brings into focus the massive benefit of increasing profitability on a continuous basis in the years before exit. It also enables you to make business decisions with a different mindset, focussing on the endgame of presenting a profitable business to buyers.

Here are a couple of ways in which Paul increased his earnings prior to sale:

- Paul effected a corporate restructure, resulting in annual savings of $200,000. The restructure cost the business $250,000 in taxation, professional costs and other expenses in the year in which it was implemented, with the savings being obtained in the following year and ongoing. So, there was a significant upfront cost to the business in effecting the restructure – indeed, it cost more than the first year's savings. However, by adding the 3 x multiple to the improved bottom line, Paul recouped significantly more upon exit.

- Paul acquired a small competing business as a 'bolt-on' acquisition. Paul's bank assisted with funding the acquisition. That 'bolt on' business brought additional earnings to Paul's Cleaning Company from day 1. Paul was then able to increase those earnings by combining the back office functions of both businesses and reducing overhead costs. By multiplying those new earnings by three upon sale, Paul created significant capital appreciation.

The responsible use of debt to fund acquisitions is a powerful way to increase your earnings and, therefore, value on sale. This is something that private equity buyers and large companies have been doing successfully for years. They select a market sector that is ripe for consolidation, buy a number of businesses in that sector with the help of bank debt, realise synergies, reduce overhead cost, and then sell. However, in my experience private and family-owned businesses are generally less inclined to progress this strategy, or when they do so poor planning means that some of them make mistakes.

There are certainly some potential risks associated with this strategy, including the risk of taking on more debt than you can handle, the risk of buying a business that does not perform as you expect, and the cultural and management challenges of integrating the new business into your existing organisation. However, if you can get it right the rewards can be huge. As with any investment decision, risk and reward go hand in hand and you need to fully understand and be comfortable with the risks before proceeding.

As food for thought, here are some reasons why private equity buyers and large companies are good at progressing this type of strategy and managing the risks:

- They understand how to put debt effectively to work on a company's balance sheet. In particular, they are not afraid of taking on the *right amount of debt,* being an amount that the business can service comfortably and that will assist with their plans to grow and exit.
- They retain experienced advisers to help them with acquisition strategies and to negotiate the best deal.
- They do not allow themselves to be consumed by the day-to-day management of the business. Instead, they keep their ear to the ground for acquisition opportunities and dedicate sufficient resources to investigating those opportunities.
- They develop deep networks within their own industries and the corporate advisory, investment banking and business broking communities. They then ensure that the people in those networks understand exactly what kind of acquisition targets they are looking for, and enlist their help in finding them.
- They pay for the best professional advice and conduct a rigorous due diligence investigation. This reduces their risk of buying a 'turkey'.
- They have a sense of urgency. In the case of private equity buyers, they are looking to grow and exit a business over a set time period in order to return money to their investors. Or, in the case of large companies, they are looking to satisfy the relentless growth expectations of the stock market. This keeps them focussed and less susceptible to distraction by non-strategic issues.

Are there any lessons that you can learn from these sophisticated operators?

Don't misrepresent your profitability

When looking to increase the earnings of your business before sale, what you must avoid at all costs is putting yourself in a position where potential buyers or their accountants allege that you have tried to massage the figures or misrepresent the profitability of your business in order to enhance the sale price.

So, there is a balancing act here – you must work hard to show the buyer that your business is profitable, but never cross the line into misrepresentation.

Some classic examples include:

- *Inappropriately running down capital expenditure, or reducing ongoing maintenance costs, in the year before sale.* Canny buyers will simply add these costs back in their valuation model, and then knock off an additional amount from the price to reflect the increased capital expenditure that will be needed after they have bought the business.

- *Killing all marketing spend in the year before sale.* This will cause fear and concern in the mind of the buyer that the earnings they are buying will not continue following the sale. There may also be a need for increased advertising or other marketing following the sale to win back brand awareness.

Even if the buyer does not pick up on these matters before the sale, if things go wrong afterwards they will certainly scour back over the records and look to use them as a basis for sending a writ your way.

Increasing the multiple

As I mentioned above, the multiple that a buyer will pay for a business is largely a factor of risk. The riskier the future of your business, the lower the multiple, and vice versa.

So, to increase the multiple upon sale, *you must reduce the buyer's perception of risk.*

And indeed, when evaluating your business, the buyer's **perception of risk** is as important as the **actual risk** in the business. You should always remember that, like beauty, risk is *'in the eye of the beholder'!*

Business risk can come in many forms, such as:

1. *customer risk* (key customers cease to buy goods or services from your business)
2. *systems risk* (internal controls and procedures are inadequate to prevent waste, error or fraud)
3. *regulatory risk* (new laws or compliance obligations increase the cost of doing business)
4. *technology risk* (new technology reduces the need for the products or services of your business)
5. *key person risk* (staff members leave with valuable knowledge, skills or relationships)
6. *supplier risk* (key suppliers cease to supply your business or materially change the price or other terms of supply)
7. *competition risk* (new competitors enter the market with a more compelling value proposition)
8. *financing risk* (interest rates increase or financing terms become more onerous)
9. *environmental risk* (the activities of your business cause contamination and associated legal and reputation issues)
10. *foreign exchange risk* (exchange rates change and affect imports or exports).

Paul's Cleaning Company – Part 2

In the case of Paul's Cleaning Company, some ways for Paul to minimise the risk of the earnings not materialising (and therefore, increasing the multiple upon sale) may be as follows:

- Consider changing the business name. One potential problem with the name 'Paul's Cleaning Company' is that it is inexorably linked to Paul. If Paul is no longer part of Paul's Cleaning Company, there may be some actual or perceived risk that the business would suffer because of this. Changing the business name will assist Paul in supporting a position that the goodwill belongs to the business and is not attached to Paul personally.

- Expand the service offering so that it is not 100 per cent reliant on cleaning services. For example, Paul could expand the business to become a broader facilities management operation. In taking this step, Paul could create new revenue streams which would mitigate against the risk of (say) a new large company significantly undercutting his prices for cleaning services. The broader service offering may also have the effect of creating a closer and more meaningful relationship with customers, which may give them less incentive to buy elsewhere.

- Ensure that key employees are bound by employment agreements, which contain robust restraint-of-trade clauses (clauses which prevent them from soliciting customers or employees, or competing with the business, for a certain period following termination of employment).

Clearly none of these changes can occur on the cusp of selling the business. They need to be identified and dealt with some time (perhaps one, two or three years) before Paul takes the business to the market for sale.

Getting the best price on sale

As a final exercise, if you are mathematically minded, think what can happen to Paul's sale price if he is able to increase *both the profits **and** the multiple.*

Say that through the initiatives referred to above Paul increases the profits of his business from $3 million to $5 million, and also increases the multiple on sale from 3 to 4. You do the maths:

Paul has increased the value of his business from $9 million to $20 million!

Or, better still, what if Paul is able to provide a credible budget and business plan to the buyer which shows profits rising to $6 million next year? He may persuade the buyer to pay that multiple based on next year's profits. Work it out – *Paul would increase the value of his business to $24 million.* And even if Paul is then required to put (say) $3 million of this extra money at risk subject to the business achieving budget next year, he is still ahead.

KEY LEARNINGS FROM THIS CHAPTER:

- Credible financial projections can help you to sell for a premium. Preparing detailed budgets in the years before sale, and demonstrating that your business has performed in accordance with those budgets, is a powerful way to support your financial projections.

- Do not become 'dazzled' by the headline valuation number. Instead, ensure that you have realistic expectations by calculating the net, after tax return that you will receive in your pocket.

- A typical multiple of three or four times EBIT means that for every $1 of additional profit you can generate, you will make $3 or $4 upon exit. Clever business owners are therefore totally focussed on maximising profitability in the years before sale.

- If you wish to increase the multiple upon sale, look at ways to reduce the *buyer's perception of risk.*

- In your quest to maximise profits before exit, do not cross the line into misrepresenting the business. The buyer will find out!

Chapter 3

Preparing for exit: the basics

In this chapter you will learn

the basic requirements to prepare your business for exit

What are the basic requirements?

This chapter addresses the basic steps that you should take to prepare your business for sale. These are good housekeeping matters that should be dealt with as an ongoing process in the months and years before exit. Later we will look at the premium value drivers over and above these basic requirements, which will help you to sell for a 'super profit'.

I have seen many business owners start a sale process without covering off the basic requirements set out in this chapter. In those cases, the outcomes included the sale falling through, the price being substantially discounted, or the sellers signing a sale agreement that was so onerous it felt like putting a big noose around their neck and kicking away the chair.

From the other side of the negotiating table, when advising buyers I have learned how to 'zoom in' quickly on the risks associated with a seller's failure to address these basics. I have then used this to help my buyer clients put pressure on the seller and negotiate substantial concessions in the sale agreement.

Remember, you may only get one chance at this.

If you take your business to market but fail to sell because you have not got the basics right, your business may become tarnished by that fact. Once you and your business have been through a failed sale process, it can be extremely difficult to regain credibility.

The basic requirements to prepare your business for sale are:
- quality financial records and reporting
- an appropriate corporate structure
- no cash or 'under the counter' transactions
- clear legal rights to key business assets
- no key customer or supplier reliance
- no major known risks

Let's now look at these in detail.

Quality financial records and reporting

When looking to acquire your business, potential buyers will have their accountants carry out some financial due diligence and prepare a valuation report (see chapter 2).

You should expect the buyer's accountants to be competent and highly motivated 'terriers', who will take great professional pride in sniffing out and hunting down problems and inconsistencies in your financial information. You might think that accountants are shy and retiring types, but believe me they get seriously excited about this stuff! Their findings will feed back into the valuation of your business, which will in turn provide the buyer with maximum ammunition to negotiate on price.

Business owners often get a nasty surprise when they realise the level of detail to which the buyer's accountants will drill down. They can also become stressed out by the relentless stream of questions and information requests that they receive. It can feel like being under the interrogation spotlight, particularly if the story told by your financials does not stack up. And, of course, by this point it is far too late to do anything about it.

Too many times I have seen business owners flummoxed, befuddled and downright red-faced when an accountant goes through their books and identifies matters such as:

- improper or inadequate provisions for bad and doubtful debts or accrued employee entitlements
- optimistic financial projections that are simply not grounded in reality
- evidence of running down capital expenditure in the years before sale in the hope of maximising the perception of profitability
- income or expenditure incorrectly allocated to the wrong year(s)
- exceptional or one-off items that are hidden or difficult to ascertain from the accounts.

How do you avoid this embarrassing outcome? The answer is simple. *Put your hand in your pocket and invest in strong accounting support.*

Sophisticated buyers of businesses normally look to see high-quality monthly and annual financial statements. The annual financial statements should at least be reviewed (if not audited) by a reputable external accountant. As indicated in the previous chapter, it is also important to demonstrate a robust annual budgeting process and regular cash flow forecasts. This not only indicates to a buyer that debtors and liquidity are being properly managed, but also provides meaningful support for your financial projections.

As a general rule of thumb, you should aim to have at least three years worth of quality historical financial information to present to prospective buyers. Ideally, that financial information should show steady increases in profitability, which will assist you and the prospective buyer to identify a growth trend in the business and give credibility to your financial projections.

If your sale transaction will be structured as the sale of shares in a company (see Chapter 6 for further details), it is also important to ensure that the company's tax compliance is up to date and in good order for review by potential buyers. Any aggressive or 'creative' tax planning from previous years will be sure to come back and bite you.

Corporate structure

In the private and family-owned business world, personal assets are unfortunately often held in the same corporate structure as the business.

In my time I have seen it all – investment portfolios, holiday homes, racehorses, luxury cars, and yachts, to name but a few. And for those business owners with unresolved matrimonial issues, another undesirable aspect is that perhaps those assets are also being used by a former (or soon to be former!) spouse who treats them as his or her property.

While there may have been good (i.e. good in the short term) reasons for doing this, holding personal assets in your business structure gives you a headache when offering your business for sale. This is because:

- you may need to extract the non-business assets from the structure before sale. This can be a complex and costly exercise and may have adverse tax consequences
- the accounts of the business will need to be normalised to reflect how they would have looked if those assets had not been part of the structure
- you will give the impression of a sloppy enterprise that has not been professionally run, with little concept of separation between your personal

and business affairs. Potential buyers may wonder – if you have been naive enough to hold your personal investments in the same corporate structure as your business, what other problems might be lurking?

Another common mistake is to have an overly complex corporate structure, with myriad different group companies, trusts, offshore subsidiaries and other weird and wonderful aspects. Structures like this can be hard to decipher and scare a buyer.

The best approach is to simplify and 'de-clutter' your corporate structure before progressing an exit strategy. Good professional advice – and particularly tax advice – is crucial before undertaking a restructure of this nature.

Cash businesses

People who run cash businesses are not only breaking the law, they are also setting themselves up in a business that will be extremely difficult to sell.

How can a prospective buyer have faith in the financials that are provided for such a business? It is pretty difficult to calculate a purchase price based on a multiple of earnings when those earnings were stuffed under the counter or in a separate till!

And, if you are the type of business person who engages in this sort of behaviour, how will a buyer ever completely trust your decency, integrity or that you have complied with your legal obligations in other areas of the business?

If you are running a cash business, take the pain now and start fully declaring your income. *You should then only look to sell the business once you have a few 'clean' years under your belt.*

Clear rights to key assets

When conducting legal due diligence on businesses for buyer clients, I often find that the sellers have not taken appropriate steps to protect the key assets of their business. This increases the buyer's perception of risk, with a corresponding negative impact upon value and sale price.

Some common examples of the failure to protect key business assets are as follows.

Failure to secure key revenue streams through long-term contracts

Many private and family-owned businesses have no contracts to secure their key revenue streams. Instead, they rely on personal relationships or the philosophy that *'this is how we have always done business'*.

Or, if such contracts do exist, they may contain prohibitions on assigning the contract (that is, transferring the contract to the buyer of your business) or otherwise entitle the customer to terminate the contract upon a change in control of your business. This means that you and the buyer would need to go 'cap in hand' to important customers before the sale and ask them to consent to the transaction. You can imagine what leverage this gives the customers!

So, when negotiating contracts at any time during the life cycle of your business, it is important that you focus on these types of clauses and ensure as far as possible that they do not inhibit a future sale.

Failure to secure long-term leases for key premises

If your business is dependent upon a particular leased site (for example, a retail location on a busy shopping strip) there may be significant value in the lease. You should therefore consider looking to secure a favourable, long-term lease from the landlord before you take the business to the market. You should also get some expert property law advice to ensure that the lease is 'marketable' to prospective acquirers of your business.

On this subject, I have seen clever entrepreneurs establish businesses in prime hospitality sites with the upfront intention of selling a couple of years after start-up. They focus their energies on negotiating a locked-in, long-term lease that is readily assignable. Having no desire to stay in the business as long-term operators, they concentrate on creating a venue that will launch with a bang and attract significant media attention in its early years. After two years or so, and once their bar or restaurant has become one of the trendiest places in town, they sell it for a premium with good ongoing security of tenure for the new owner.

Failure to protect important intellectual property rights

Properly protecting your intellectual property rights through patents, trademarks and the like can certainly be costly and time-consuming. However, with the endgame of sale in mind, the really exciting thing about doing this is that it allows you to create a true barrier to entry for your competitors. Particularly for technology-based businesses, registering a patent gives you a *legal monopoly* position in relation to that technology. How good is that!

Trademark protection is equally as important. I once knew a large company which, immediately before selling its business, realised that one of its much smaller competitors not only traded under exactly the same name, but had also registered that name as a trademark in many countries throughout the world.

The large company ended up having to pay a significant sum of money to the smaller company to purchase the trademark. Failure to protect their intellectual property assets cost them dearly.

Key customer or key supplier reliance

Any merger or acquisition brings with it the risk that customers and suppliers will re-appraise their relationship with the business and possibly move elsewhere.

And when your business is heavily reliant on one key customer or supplier, the risk for the buyer is magnified dramatically.

Once a potential buyer becomes aware of how reliant your business is on those customers or suppliers, that buyer may decide that a better strategy is simply to try and target your customers or suppliers direct, rather than acquiring your business. Or, they might seek a substantial discount to the price to reflect the risk of those customers or suppliers departing.

If your business is reliant on a small number of key customers or suppliers, a strategy should be put in place to minimise that reliance before taking the business to market, even if this is likely to take some time to implement effectively.

Succession story – Deepak

Deepak owned a business which had an exclusive licence to import and sell a prestigious brand of luggage and handbags. Deepak had enjoyed a close and mutually profitable relationship with the overseas owner of the brand for many years. His goal was to grow and exit the business over a five-year period before his 60th birthday.

Recognising that a significant amount of the value of his business came via the licence agreement with the overseas brand-owner, Deepak put in place a long-term strategy that enabled him to renegotiate the licence agreement one year before he intended to take the business to the market for sale.

When the time came to renegotiate, Deepak made certain concessions to the brand owner, in return for securing a long-term agreement that would be attractive to a potential buyer. Deepak also made sure that the licence agreement was transferable to a buyer approved by the brand owner (who, importantly, agreed to an obligation not to unreasonably withhold or delay that approval).

In order to reduce the reliance of the business upon the licence agreement, Deepak also put in place a strategy of expanding the product range for his shops. He also ensured that his key personnel were introduced to the licensor, to reduce the dependence on his personal relationship.

Major known risks

If there is a known risk issue in your business, you should take steps to fix that issue before offering your business for sale, even if there is some cost associated with this.

One example is litigation claims. If your business is being sued for any reason, or if someone has threatened to sue, this will increase the buyer's perception of risk and cause them concern, even if you believe that you have a good defence to the claim.

You are generally better off to settle the claim before taking the business to the market, even if you settle for an amount that is greater than your 'best case' scenario. Litigation is a contingent liability that scares buyers.

Environmental risks

Of all categories of business risk, I have seen environmental risks kill more sale transactions than any other single item. For this reason, I wanted to tell you about these risks in some detail.

Environmental risks may take a wide variety of forms. For example, they may be associated with contaminated land, ground gases, groundwater contamination, smoke and other emissions, asbestos materials in buildings and industrial processes that use chemicals or other environmentally harmful materials.

It is not just actual, concrete environmental liabilities that can kill a deal. *Sometimes even the perception or fear of environmental risk can 'spook' a buyer.*

I remember once working with a buyer on the proposed purchase of shares in a manufacturing company which engaged in highly regulated and polluting industrial processes. The directors of the buyer were so concerned about environmental risks that they not only examined the manufacturing sites currently operated by the target company, but also made detailed investigations in relation to each and every site that it had operated in the last twenty years. Their concern was that if those sites had been contaminated by the company, then that liability could still come back to bite the company after they had bought it. Unfortunately, the seller did not have good current environmental processes or records, let alone in relation to historical sites. This made the buyer extremely nervous and they eventually decided not to proceed.

Why are environmental issues so scary for buyers?

One reason is the legal exposures, which can be broad and onerous. These include liability for clean-up, the stigma and consequent reduction in land value, and increasingly severe fines and penalties.

There is also the risk of claims by third parties who suffer loss as a result of the contamination, such as employees whose health is affected or neighbouring landowners. Liability for environmental issues can, in certain circumstances, go 'up the tree' to the ultimate holding company or attach personally to directors of the offending company.

Perhaps most importantly, there is also the reputational risk for prospective buyers who will not want to be associated with a well-publicised environmental or public health catastrophe. These reputational concerns are top of mind for large companies (who may otherwise perhaps pay the best price for your business).

If there are any actual or perceived environmental issues in your business, it is important that you don't try to downplay them. Instead, the better approach is generally that you:

1. Review and audit the environmental issues in good time before implementing any exit strategy.

2. Ensure that appropriate, up-to-date written procedures (which can be disclosed to the buyer during their due diligence investigations) are in place to reduce environmental risk going forward. Ensure that sufficient resources are devoted to ensuring that those procedures are complied with and records of compliance are kept.

3. Obtain an environmental site assessment to understand the extent of the contamination, what action is required, the most feasible options available to remediate and an estimated cost and time frame for remediation. Do not scrimp on the cost or scope of the environmental site assessment. The environmental site assessment will give no comfort to a buyer if the extent of the testing was inadequate.

4. Once the environmental site assessment has been obtained, give thought to which issues can or should be remediated immediately. If you make the decision to remediate early in the process it can often cost you less. This is because you can opt for the most cost-effective (but perhaps slower) remediation options, instead of the quick fix. If you remediate, always have a plan with clear objectives before committing to the costs involved.

5. Always obtain another environmental site assessment following remediation in order to demonstrate that the clean-up has been effective.

6. If there has been any correspondence or other dealings with governments or environmental regulators in relation to the site or the business, provide full disclosure to potential buyers.

7. If contaminated land is leased, carefully review the lease and ascertain whether you or the landlord is responsible for clean-up (and to what standard). And, always remember that even if the landlord has a contractual responsibility to clean up under a lease, this may not absolve the polluter from legal exposures such as fines, penalties and clean-up obligations.

KEY LEARNINGS FROM THIS CHAPTER:

- Preparing your business for exit may take several months or years. Plan ahead to avoid having to progress your exit strategy prematurely.

- Remember the basic requirements:
    - quality financial records and reporting
    - an appropriate corporate structure
    - no cash or 'under the counter' transactions
    - clear legal rights to key business assets
    - no key customer or supplier reliance
    - no major known risks

- Expect potential buyers and their accountants to conduct an extremely rigorous due diligence investigation on your business. Be well prepared for this, or you will find yourself embarrassed and negotiating from a position of weakness.

- Environmental risks can kill transactions.

Chapter 4

Premium value drivers

In this chapter you will learn

**to identify the 'big four' premium value drivers
and how to create them in your business**

Premium value drivers

In this chapter I will reveal to you the premium value drivers in private and family-owned businesses.

These are the additional factors over and above the basic requirements described in Chapter 3. If you can demonstrate these factors to a buyer, they will give your business the best chance to stand out from the crowd and be sold for a substantial premium.

So what are these elusive premium value drivers?

Based on the successful transactions that I have seen in my career, the big four 'slam dunks' are:

1. lack of principal dependency (and with key personnel locked in)
2. creating a sustainable competitive advantage
3. strong governance systems
4. being a strategic acquisition target for your competitors.

Let's consider each of the big four in detail.

Premium value driver number 1: Lack of principal dependency

Principal dependency means the over-reliance of a business upon its owner(s). Is this a feature of your business? If so, you are not alone – it is extremely common in private and family-owned businesses.

Principal dependency can arise in a number of ways. It can occur through you being the only person who holds the main customer relationships. Or perhaps you are the only person who has an intimate understanding of the core technology or key systems of the business. Or maybe the loyalty of the staff is based primarily on a longstanding personal relationship with you and your family.

Principal dependency is a particularly common feature of businesses that have been created and grown by an entrepreneur from the ground up. Typically, these business owners are very passionate about their business and its products or services. This passion, together with an engaging personality and good leadership skills, has resulted in the recruitment and retention of a hardworking and loyal workforce.

These business owners have also generally worked extremely hard to grow the business through its early years via networking and relationship-based marketing. (There was probably not a big enough marketing budget to do anything else!)

Does any of this sound like you and your business?

The factors set out above are, in one sense, extremely positive aspects of an entrepreneurial business. However, the other side of the equation is that such a business is also likely to be highly dependent on you, its owner. If you retired from your executive position or were hit by the proverbial bus, it would be difficult for the business to survive, let alone grow and thrive.

Some of the problems that may be faced by an outwardly successful (yet principal dependent) business are:

- a business owner who has become tired and stressed out by carrying the emotional burden of the ongoing success of the business alone
- customers who are starting to receive sub-standard service because the business owner is too busy to look after them properly, but has not effectively introduced other staff members into the customer relationship
- a business owner who has become so deeply focussed on day-to-day activities that it has become difficult to step back and take a more strategic view
- a business where the systems and procedures are contained in the business owner's head only, and which is therefore becoming increasingly inefficient as it grows.

The buyer's perspective

When a potential buyer looks critically at your business, various concerns are associated with key person dependency. Their concerns may include the following:

- When I acquire the business, will the customers follow?
- Will the staff be loyal to me, the new owner?
- Which staff members hold the corporate memory of the business?
- Who understands the systems, processes and other idiosyncrasies of the business?
- Have the relationships between the business and yourself or your family been run on a strictly commercial, arm's-length basis?

Some common ways that buyers seek to reduce the risks associated with key person dependency include:

- Reducing the purchase price to reflect the key person risk. *I have seen significant sums of money knocked straight off the sale price of otherwise strong businesses for exactly this reason.*
- Paying a smaller amount of the purchase price upfront, with a major part of the purchase price to be at risk and paid at a later date, depending on future performance.
- Requiring you, the owner, to keep working in the business as an employee or consultant for a lengthy period of time following the sale.
- Imposing painful and ugly restraint-of-trade obligations (i.e. obligations not to compete with the business or solicit clients or employees for a certain period of time following the sale). While every seller of a business should expect to give restraint-of-trade obligations, the broadest and nastiest of them all are imposed on sellers whose businesses are heavily dependent on them personally.
- Ensure that systemic changes are made to the business, at your cost, before sale. I once advised the buyer of a retail business where the detailed systems and procedures of that business were contained only in the seller's head. As a condition of buying the business, my clever client insisted that the seller prepare a detailed procedures manual, and also provide warranties in the sale agreement that the procedures manual was complete and accurate. The time and cost incurred by the seller in preparing that manual, not to mention the emotional stress of doing so under pressure in the weeks before sale, were significant.

43

How to reduce principal dependency

Having identified principal dependency, the difficulty (and where most business owners fail) is in actually doing something about this.

Here are some of the reasons given to me by business owners for failing to minimise principal dependency:

- *'I would like to give more responsibility to my staff but they simply won't step up. They just don't care about the business like I do.'*
- *'I know that I need to appoint a good manager. It's just that I can't recruit the right person. Or, when I do find a decent candidate, they generally want too much money or resign after 12 months.'*
- *'How can I transition my key client relationships to the sales team? My customers have been dealing with me for 20 years. They trust me, and we both enjoy the business relationship.'*

If you feel that any of these reasons apply to you, and even if there is some truth in them, you really need to see them for what they are: excuses not to recognise and confront important issues in your business. *Your inability to address these issues is not only poor management in the short term, but will also cost you significant money on exit.*

If your staff are unable to 'step up' there should only be two outcomes – either those people need to be given the support and training to take the next step, or they are not the right people for the job and their employment should be terminated (which should only occur after you have received proper employment law advice).

Rather than blaming your inability to recruit good staff on the market or the unrealistic expectations of job seekers, you should hold up the mirror to your business and the role, responsibilities and remuneration package that you offer. You should then reflect on how, within reason, these could be made more attractive to prospective employees. Perhaps it is the perceived lack of career progression (because you will always rule the roost) that is putting off prospective employees?

If customers continue to liaise directly with you, this simply means that you must work harder at improving your delegation skills or implementing processes to ensure that key staff members undertake an appropriate amount of the customer-facing work.

Confronting these issues can be difficult, as the underlying reasons often have a deep-seated emotional or psychological aspect.

These issues have perhaps arisen through your fear (or would *paranoia* be a better word?!) that staff will make a mistake or will never do things quite as well as you do. That fear may then have warped into your need to control everything and everyone in your business to an unhealthy degree.

Or, these issues may have arisen out of your inability to let go of the 'baby' that you have created, nurtured and cherished over many years. Applying the mirror test to your business can provide a reality check – has that cute little baby grown into a delinquent teenager?

Due to the deeply personal nature of the issues, reducing principal dependency in a private or family-owned business is generally not a quick fix. The solution is often a multi-faceted one that needs to be implemented over time and requires cultural and behavioural change, which must occur from the top down. Some aspects to this solution might be letting go, developing your staff and ensuring that key personnel are 'locked in'.

- *Letting go*

  Working with a business coach or psychologist, or joining a CEO group where you can discuss issues openly and confidentially with peers, can be a powerful way to obtain objective feedback on issues such as the inability to delegate or how to groom and develop your senior management team.

  This mentoring can be extremely effective as a precursor to implementing change to reduce principal dependency as part of a long-term succession strategy.

  It pays to remember that the most successful business owners are the ones who put the right people around them. Indeed, there is one school of thought which says that recruiting and retaining the right people is the only thing that a great leader needs to do. Those good people will then take care of the rest. And if you feel insecure about this, ***get over it!*** Remember that the right people will only make you look better anyway.

  A friend of mine has lived by this philosophy for years. As the owner and CEO of a highly profitable business, his number one focus is *recruitment* – i.e. getting the very best people around him. He then concentrates on strategy, *without getting involved in any operational aspects of the business.* He spends a lot of time one-on-one with each of his senior managers to support them, motivate them, and obtain their 'buy in' to his strategic vision. But then, he leaves it up to those managers to decide how they will do their bit to achieve that vision. And if one of his managers then doesn't deliver the goods, he is rigorous in performance managing them.

- *Developing staff*

  You should ensure that all key staff have a documented career progression plan. This plan should be discussed and agreed between you (or your human resources manager) and those staff members, and regularly updated.

The plan should set out the short to medium-term goals of the staff member, and the key performance indicators that they need to achieve in order to reach those goals. As part of the plan, the staff member should understand the direction in which the business is going and what you need from them.

To make the career progression plan work, you must ensure that there is continual open and honest communication between yourself and the staff member. This means being able to deliver feedback and communicate expectations about performance in a way that is helpful and constructive, without shying away from difficult issues.

A career progression plan of this nature has the dual purpose of ensuring that employees are challenged, engaged and continually developing their skill set, and also reducing the dependency of the business on you personally.

I have seen these plans used to great effect both in my own business and the businesses of my clients. The staff member feels valued and can see a clear path to career progression, and you can start trusting that person to undertake additional and more complex functions. *Indeed – challenging your staff and giving them greater opportunities is usually the quickest way to find out if they are the right person for the job!*

When grooming and developing staff, it is crucial that you do not simply shift the dependency from yourself to one (or a small number of) key staff member(s). This won't solve your business succession issues – in fact, it will add to them. This is because you will give those people significant leverage to either 'scupper' a sale to a third party or, alternatively, to acquire the business themselves on very favourable terms. The trick is to ensure that you are always spreading the important duties and responsibilities among a number of people in the business, and that internal successors are trained and available to step into your senior team's shoes if necessary.

- *Ensuring key staff are 'locked in'*

  If you are going to transition your business from being principal-dependent, it is crucial that your senior staff are not only well motivated and have a transparent career path, but also that they are 'locked in'.

  This means that:
  - They have a competitive salary or remuneration package. Ideally, that package would be structured in a way that gives them an incentive to

assist in growing the business and share the risk and reward of this with you.

o They have a robust employment contract that adequately protects your confidential information, intellectual property and customer and employee relationships.

It is also useful for the employment contracts to contain full-form job descriptions. In this way, when it comes time to sell, prospective buyers will be able to review these contracts and clearly understand the executive functions of your senior management team.

It would be extremely dangerous for you to transition relationships and other responsibilities to your senior management team without locking them in as described above. Senior employees who are disgruntled and who could leave tomorrow and set up in competition will always jeopardise your business succession plan.

I recall once assisting a buyer client to conduct legal due diligence investigations on a potential acquisition target. Our investigations identified that a manager of the business, who had no equity share, held most of the key customer relationships. That manager was employed under the terms of a flimsy offer letter that he had signed many years ago when he joined the business as a graduate. That offer letter allowed him to terminate his employment at any time on two weeks' notice and did not contain any post-termination restraint-of-trade obligations (i.e. there were no obligations on him not to compete with the business, or solicit customers or employees, for a period of time following the termination of his employment).

Understandably, the buyer insisted on the manager signing a new employment contract as a condition of the acquisition. The buyer also insisted on being given the opportunity to speak with the manager at an early stage, to ascertain whether he would be keen to stay on in the role. The manager of course then realised that he had significant leverage in the sale process. He ended up signing the new employment contract, but only after the buyer had offered a significant pay rise and an attractive new bonus structure. Of course, the buyer then simply adjusted the purchase price downwards to reflect this additional cost.

Premium value driver number 2: Sustainable competitive advantage

Businesses which have a *sustainable competitive advantage* generally sell for a super-profit.

Having a sustainable competitive advantage means that your business has something that is unique and difficult or costly for your competitors to emulate. Think of Microsoft's control of personal computer operating systems, or the massive brand power of Cadbury in the chocolate market.

In his seminal article 'What is Strategy'[1], Michael E Porter said that having a sustainable competitive advantage is achieved through strategic positioning. He wrote:

Strategic positioning means performing different activities from rivals, or performing similar activities in different ways.

Having a sustainable competitive advantage is different from running an efficient business. Running an efficient business just reduces your costs and increases competitiveness in your market. The ultimate beneficiary of that increased efficiency is therefore the consumer (who benefits from lower prices) and not you, the business owner. An example of this would be the trend of western businesses achieving savings through outsourcing their manufacturing function to certain Asian countries where the cost of labour is cheaper.

'OK, but how does this apply to me?' you may think. *'My little business is nothing like Cadbury or Microsoft.'*

Well, it applies to your business in exactly the same way. Some examples of a sustainable competitive advantage that you might create for your business could include:

- offering greater depth of products in a limited range, when your competitors are offering less depth in a broader range
- providing a more basic, trimmed-down service offering than your competitors at a lower cost (or alternatively, providing a fuller service offering than your competitors at a higher cost)
- providing a broad range of products to a niche sector of the market (for example, high net-worth individuals or people residing in your geographic region)

- creating a novel patented technology that performs a function differently to the products of your competitors.

Porter cites IKEA as an example of a company that created a sustainable competitive advantage. IKEA caters for families who want stylish furniture at a low price – something that furniture stores have not catered well for historically. IKEA sacrifices high levels of service for low-cost, ready-to-assemble furniture. It does not deliver its products; customers collect them from a warehouse next to the store. IKEA also provides additional services that its competitors do not – for example, childcare facilities and a coffee shop.

Creating a sustainable competitive advantage means that your business must not try to be all things to all people. *In fact, the exact opposite should be true.* You should:

- identify what your business excels at (or could excel at)
- focus on being a 'superstar' in that area
- ignore other opportunities which, while profitable in the short term, are a distraction from that focus.

This concept was explored in 'The Core Competence of the Corporation' by CK Prahalad and Gary Hamel[2]. They argued that a business should invest its best people and resources in its core competencies, being the things that it can do uniquely well and that are difficult for competitors to emulate quickly. Excelling in those core competencies may then provide access to a broad range of markets. They give the following example:

> *Consider 3M's competence with sticky tape. In dreaming up businesses as diverse as Post-it notes, magnetic tape, photographic film, pressure-sensitive tapes and coated abrasives, the company has brought to bear widely shared competencies in substrates, coatings and adhesives and devised various ways to combine them. Indeed, 3M has invested consistently in them. What seems to be an extremely diversified portfolio of businesses belies a few shared core competencies.*

Do you recall earlier in this book I mentioned the importance of preparing good historical financial information as a basic requirement before selling? Well, whilst that advice remains sound, here's a 'head shift' for you – to most people who are looking to buy your business, *a true sustainable competitive advantage is preferable to solid historical performance.*

This is because the buyer is not buying your history.

To the buyer, the sustainable competitive advantage represents the future earning potential of your business. *At the end of the day, this is what they will pay for.*

As an action point, try writing down the true point(s) of difference or sustainable competitive advantage(s) of your business. When asked to do this, most people will confidently write down a list of five to ten points which are really just generic marketing statements or 'me too' strategies. When you then ask them to include only the factors that make their business *truly unique*, their list becomes much shorter!

Take my own industry, the legal industry, as an example. If you review the websites of most commercial law firms you will be amazed at how similar they all are. Every single one offers high levels of technical expertise, formidable experience in a range of different transactions or disputes, personal service, and an assurance that their firm will provide practical commercial solutions and not just legalistic advice. Whilst the law firms might try and sell these attributes as 'points of difference', they are in fact totally generic.

There is no single bright idea that I can offer which will provide your business with a sustainable competitive advantage.

All I can say is that I have seen it happen – the businesses with this elusive 'X factor' sell for more every single time.

And this occurs even if those businesses don't display some of the other desirable attributes that I have mentioned to you in this book.

Here's a challenge – take an hour out of your day tomorrow and think about how you could create a sustainable competitive advantage in your business. Better still, workshop it with a colleague or two. Put a note in your diary to make yourself commit. And if you say you don't have the time, get up an hour earlier and do it first thing in the morning. It won't kill you!

Premium value driver number 3: Strong governance systems

I cannot over-emphasise to you the fear that buyers have about the risk of an unforseen catastrophic event occurring in your business after they have bought it. This is the stuff that haunts their nightmares and causes them to wake up in a cold sweat.

So, to create a premium value driver, you should show the buyer that you have already addressed these risks through *strong governance systems.* Another benefit of implementing these systems is that they provide potent evidence that your business is a viable living organism in its own right, which can survive without your day-to-day input. So again, we are back to the theme of reducing principal dependency.

Strong governance starts at the top level with an effective board and management structure. It then flows down through the business to include detailed systems and processes for managing operational risk.

The truly ghoulish risk issues that can turn a good acquisition into an X-rated horror movie include major fraud, environmental hazards, problems in manufacturing systems which produce dangerous goods, health and safety issues, and significant negligence claims.

If these issues rise up like zombies from the crypt following an acquisition, the damage to the buyer can be huge. Even if the buyer did not acquire the shares in your company and therefore did not take on these liabilities directly (see Chapter 6) they will still be saddled with the reputational issues and consequent loss of business. They will also carry the burden of fixing up your systems and procedures to ensure that this can never happen again.

Imagine that you are a senior executive of a large company who is recommending to his or her Board to buy your business. That executive can probably live with the risk that the earnings of your business may not be as strong as anticipated, or that a couple of customers may fall away. But what if your business were to suffer a catastrophic event after it has been acquired? The buyer, and the career of the executive who recommended the acquisition, may never survive.

I once attended a conference where 'Aussie John' Symond from Aussie Home Loans was a participant in a panel discussion. The panellists were asked the question *'what issue do you wake up worrying about in the middle of the night?'* John answered that for him, the big issue is the risk of a 'bad apple' employee committing a fraud which is not picked up by Aussie's strong internal control systems, and which irreparably damages the brand that he has grown and nurtured for many years. John's answer then led to a very interesting panel discussion about the importance of having strong procedures to reduce this risk.

Private and family-owned businesses are notorious for their weak or non-existent governance systems. For example, the KPMG and Family Business Australia Survey of Family Businesses 2009 found that:

- only 28 per cent of respondents had established formal family councils
- only one-third of respondents had a board or other formal governing body
- a whopping 43 per cent of respondents said that they rely on less formal structures.

The same survey found that just under half of the respondents had a business risk plan and only 34 per cent had a technology contingency plan.

So, if you have effective governance systems in your business, this will create a *powerful point of difference* that will set you apart from your competitors and serve you well on exit.

The question of what constitutes appropriate governance will vary significantly from business to business. This is not an area where 'one size fits all'. Clearly, the detailed and perhaps cumbersome governance systems of a large public company will be very different to those of a small owner-managed business.

To help you start thinking about what systems might be appropriate in your business, some good ones that I have seen used in other private and family-owned businesses are described below.

Operational committees

Even if your business is small, it can be effective to establish a committee to deal with operational risk.

Mercanti Electrics

Let's take the example of Mercanti Electrics, which is a second-generation family-owned electrical contracting business. The family has recently been approached by a competitor, which is considering making an offer to buy the business.

Three years ago, Mercanti Electrics put in place a risk management committee to monitor operational risk in relation to the business, including health and safety issues.

The committee meets every month with a simple standing agenda and comprises staff members of varying levels of seniority from all parts of the business. The responsibility to convene and chair the meetings is given to mid-level staff members on a revolving basis. The purpose of the committee is to review and consider risk issues and make recommendations to the business owners. Minutes are prepared following each meeting, and these are provided to the business owners on a timely basis for consideration at their monthly board meetings. The business owners review and discuss the minutes, liaise with the committee as appropriate and use this as a basis to implement change on an ongoing basis.

A simple procedure like this creates various benefits for the Mercanti family when negotiating the sale of the business. Through reviewing the folder of risk management committee meeting minutes, the prospective buyer will gain comfort that:

- operational and health and safety risks are taken very seriously in this business

- staff are actively involved in aspects of managing the business that fall outside their day-to-day duties

- the management of operational risk is not the sole responsibility of the Mercanti family. When they move on following the sale, there will remain an effective system in place to monitor and address these issues.

Of course, operational committees of this nature should not necessarily be limited to risk management. A formal process of meetings and minutes can be useful for various other aspects of the business, including sales meetings or divisional management meetings.

A proper management board with external representation

Of the businesses that I have seen successfully grow and exit, a strikingly common feature is that many of them have a *formal board or management committee which contains at least one external person*. That person may be a professional director, an industry expert, or a trusted professional adviser.

The benefits of a formal board structure with some independent representation are twofold. The first is the ongoing benefit of a functional forum for making decisions and receiving objective feedback. The second is the perception of strong governance that this creates in the minds of potential buyers, who will examine your board minutes as part of their due diligence investigations.

Or, if your business is not large enough to support a structure of this nature, you should at least consider getting some external perspective from another source – for example by joining a CEO group or working with a business coach, executive mentor, or other trusted adviser.

Without some external perspective, the management of private and family-owned business can be ineffective. It can be difficult for you to keep your objectivity or put aside personal interests, or to confront issues that may have an impact on close personal or family relationships.

Business coach Alan Rodway has described this conundrum as follows:

> At the boardroom table of a family company, vested interests lurk beneath the surface of many commercial decisions. Take a proposal to buy a new IT system. The 60-plus year old patriarch won't want to buy it – he is retiring soon so why should he dilute his profits? But his 30 year old son will want to buy the best, perhaps with little regard for whether the benefits will justify the expense, and particularly whilst dad is still around to wear half the cost! How can these two people, with their respective agendas, make a sensible decision that is in the best interests of the company?

While ever-increasing liabilities for directors are making it harder and more expensive to find good people to sit on public company boards, from what I have seen this issue does not translate to the private business world. It is certainly quite possible for you to find candidates for board positions who can add a lot of value and who do not 'charge like a wounded bull'.

When selecting a candidate for a board position, ensure that you choose someone with whom you have a good personal connection and who is fired up by your business. A good tip is then only to appoint them for a fixed period – say 12 months. If things don't work out, it can be awkward and embarrassing to have to dismiss your independent director. But by appointing them for a fixed period, you can both walk away and save face if necessary. Or, if things go well, you can simply extend their contract.

Premium value driver number 4: Businesses that are strategic acquisition targets for their competitors

When looking to sell your business for the highest price, you should give thought to which buyer is the most likely to pay that price.

So, who might that buyer be? There is really no hard and fast rule about this.

However, as a useful generality, *the buyer who will pay the highest price is often a competitor.*

This is because a competitor will derive most value from your business through realising synergies with their own business.

The attraction of your business to a competitor may be on a number of levels, such as:

- the ability to reduce overheads by merging back-office functions such as accounts, human resources and administration
- access to new customers or revenue streams
- the ability to create barriers to entry or increase profitability through vertical integration (the acquisition of businesses that have different, but related, processes or offerings)
- access to new distribution channels for existing products or services
- the ability to sell new products or services through existing distribution channels.

In his excellent book *Invest to Exit*[3], global serial entrepreneur Dr. Tom McKaskill argues that conventional valuation techniques can greatly undervalue a business which has assets or capabilities that can be used by a competitor to make a lot of money. So when preparing your business for sale, you should focus your energies on identifying strategic buyers and working out how to make your business more attractive to them. There is an interesting interview with McKaskill and his partner Katalin Johnson, which further expands on this concept, at the end of this book.

In *Invest to Exit,* McKaskill gives various examples of businesses that he personally grew and sold to strategic buyers, which broke the mould of the conventional three times or four times EBIT multiple.

One of those businesses was Pioneer Computer Systems, a software business that was bought by a competitor for ten times the prior year's EBIT. The buyer was much larger than Pioneer Computer Systems and was deliberately sought out by Pioneer because they were a good strategic fit. In particular, the buyer had:

- large well-established distribution networks (much larger than Pioneer's) which gave them the opportunity to make significant additional profits by selling Pioneer's products through those networks
- joint venture partners and funding in place to launch a massive push for the product in a new market.

In the case of Pioneer Computer Systems, the buyer was not so much concerned about the historical profits (of lack thereof) of the business. But they were willing to pay handsomely for the core technology and the opportunities that it would create for them.

On certain occasions, I have also seen trade buyers and their owners 'fall in love' with a target business. And as we all know, those who are in the first throes of a love affair are rarely able to think rationally!

Just like when homebuyers pay a silly price for their dream home, you can sometimes extract a significant premium from a trade buyer who has become emotionally attached to your business. The reasons for this emotional attachment may be many and varied. They can include a long-term admiration for your brand or products or services, or the satisfaction of taking a strong competitor out of the market.

Once you understand the concept of turning your business into a strategic acquisition target, your approach and attitude to competitors (especially large companies with the deepest pockets) can change dramatically. You will ensure that you do not burn bridges or create an unnecessarily hostile relationship with them.

Indeed, if a civil business relationship can be developed over the years, this will assist you to understand what is attractive to your competitors when they are looking to buy. It will also make it much easier for you to make or receive an approach if there is already a relationship of mutual respect.

From a legal perspective, a final word of warning is that you should not 'buddy up' with your competitors to the extent that you risk engaging in serious unlawful conduct such as price fixing or 'carving up' the market between you. A good understanding of the basic principles of competition law is important for any business owner, but even more so for those who seek to develop a relationship with their competitors.

KEY LEARNINGS FROM THIS CHAPTER:

- Seek to create one or more of the following premium value drivers:
    - lack of principal dependency (and with key personnel locked in)
    - sustainable competitive advantage
    - strong governance systems
    - being a strategic acquisition target for your competitors.

- If you are struggling with reducing the dependency of the business on yourself, consider joining a CEO group or working with a business coach or psychologist to talk through these issues.

- Remember that, to a buyer, a true sustainable competitive advantage may be more desirable than solid historical financials. It represents the future earning potential of your business.

- Buyers are frightened about the possibility of catastrophic risk events occurring after they have bought the business. Strong governance systems will help reduce this fear.

- Develop relationships with your competitors. They may be the buyers who will pay the most for your business.

---

1   Michael E. Porter 1996 'What is Strategy', *Harvard Business Review,* Nov/Dec. Copyright 1996 by the Harvard Business School Publishing Corporation; all rights reserved. Reprinted by permission of Harvard Business Review.

2   CK Prahalad and Gary Hamel 1990 'The Core Competence of the Corporation', *Harvard Business Review,* May/June. Copyright 1990 by the Harvard Business School Publishing Corporation; all rights reserved. Reprinted by permission of Harvard Business Review.

3   Tom McKaskill 2009 'Invest to Exit', *Breakthrough Publications.*

Chapter 5

Slow and steady: the staged succession

In this chapter you will learn

the upsides and downsides of the staged succession

and

the importance of clear rules to govern co-ownership

The Staged Succession

This chapter examines the exit strategy that I have named 'staged succession'.

A staged succession occurs when you sell your interest in a business over time, generally to the existing senior management team.

Staged successions commonly occur in family-owned businesses, where the parents own the business and sell it down gradually to their children over a number of years. It allows the children to buy the business in more manageable 'chunks'. It also allows the parents to transition gradually out of their executive roles and gives the children time to be groomed to take over those roles.

That said, staged succession is not exclusively the domain of family-owned business. I have seen this strategy used successfully in many non-family scenarios – particularly where there is a need to preserve the ongoing culture and client relationships of the business.

In particular, it can be a sound strategy in service industries with significant human capital and which are dependent on deep personal relationships (such as recruitment, accounting and consulting).

Let's use an extended case study to illustrate some of the issues associated with a staged succession.

High Quality Fasteners

Here is the story to date:

- High Quality Fasteners manufactures, imports and distributes bolts and fasteners for the construction industry.

- Stuart is the sole shareholder and managing director of High Quality Fasteners. He established the business 15 years ago with his redundancy package from a big corporate, initially operating out of his garden shed.

- High Quality Fasteners is now a substantial and profitable business, employing 50 people and turning over $30 million per annum.

- Stuart is 59 years of age. He is currently in good health, but is losing the impetus to drive the business like he used to. He would like to slow down and pursue other interests in the next three to five years.

- Stuart has lived a good lifestyle in recent years. He has not saved much money and has instead relied on the value of the business to fund his lifestyle in retirement.

- Stuart has two children, Jim and Tony.

- Jim works in the High Quality Fasteners business as the operations manager. He is in his late thirties and has a young family and significant financial commitments.

- Tony is two years younger, and a successful doctor. He has informed Stuart that he has no interest in working in, or acquiring ownership of, the family business.

- Stuart has identified Jim as a potential successor for the CEO role.

- Jim has expressed an interest in acquiring High Quality Fasteners from Stuart.

- While he earns a good salary in his role as operations manager, Jim does not have the available funds to purchase the business outright.

Stuart has proposed a staged succession whereby Jim will buy out his interest in the business over five years. Each year, he will have the option to acquire 20 per cent of Stuart's equity in High Quality Fasteners.

It is proposed that Stuart will continue to work full-time in the business for the next three years and then reduce his hours and hand over day-to-day management to Jim. Stuart plans to retire once he has sold the remaining 20 per cent interest in five years' time.

Pros and cons of a staged succession

The possible upsides of a staged succession for Stuart may be as follows:

- Jim already knows the business, its customers and suppliers.

- It reduces the risk that Jim will leave to progress other career options.

- It allows for continuity of the culture of the business upon transition to Jim.

- It allows Stuart to 'slow down' gradually over time and to participate in future value created in the business.

- Buying in stages makes funding easier for Jim.

- Because Jim knows the business, he is unlikely to require as many warranties and indemnities from Stuart in the sale agreement as a third party buyer would. Stuart may therefore exit the business 'cleaner' than if he sold to a third party.

The possible downsides of a staged succession for Stuart may be as follows:

- Stuart would not realise the full value of his interest in the business in one upfront payment.

- The control and operational dynamic in the business will change over the five-year period. Stuart has a strong personality and has always 'ruled the roost' at High Quality Fasteners – can he deal with this transition on an emotional and practical level?

- Jim could change his mind or wish to accept another job offer part-way through acquiring the business.

- Jim's performance could drop off part-way through acquiring the business.

- Tony could claim that he has been poorly treated because Jim has 'inherited' more of the family wealth than he.

- Jim may not be able to pay top dollar given his personal financial situation.

Many of these potential downsides can be mitigated or eliminated through proper planning, including an appropriately drafted shareholders agreement. Please see below for more detailed discussion on these aspects.

In addition, the question of Jim's ability (or rather, inability!) to pay for the business may potentially be addressed through debt funding. Certain banks are very familiar with this type of transaction and are able to offer creative and attractive funding packages.

Price

A key issue for Stuart and Jim in the context of the staged succession is the sale price for each 20 per cent block of shares.

Stuart's position may be that Jim should pay the market value of each block of shares on the date that he buys them. That value could be calculated in accordance with a pre-agreed formula (for example, 3 x EBIT of the previous financial year, less net debt) or determined by an independent accountant each year.

However, Jim's position may be to argue, *'Why should I pay for an increase in value that I have created?'* In other words, if the increase in the value of the business over the next five years is primarily due to Jim's efforts, why should this be factored into the price that he must pay Stuart? Jim may instead argue that each subsequent 20 per cent block of shares should be valued as at the *date upon which he acquired the first 20 per cent.*

Ultimately, there will be a commercial negotiation and a compromise struck (maybe Jim would only be required to pay for half of the increase in value created over the five-year purchase period).

This type of negotiation can often be extremely delicate. If Jim pushes too hard, he may make Stuart feel like an old 'has been' whose contribution will not be valued over the next five years. But if Stuart digs his heels in, Jim may feel exploited and look for opportunities elsewhere. And whose side will Martha, Stuart's wife and Jim's mother, take?!

Conduct of the business during the staged succession period

A key feature of the staged succession is that Stuart and Jim will be co-owners of High Quality Fasteners for a five-year period. At the beginning of that period, Stuart will be the majority owner. However, as he gradually sells down his interest, Jim will become the majority owner. Like a pendulum, the balance of power will therefore swing slowly from Stuart to Jim.

It is therefore important for Stuart and Jim to put in place a shareholders agreement as a clear rule book for the business throughout the full swing of the pendulum.

As the name suggests, a shareholders agreement is an agreement between the shareholders in a private company, which governs how the business will be run and contains mechanisms to deal with shareholders coming and going, key business decisions, dividend policies and board and shareholder meetings. Chapter 9 contains further detail on these agreements.

The Shareholders Agreement

From Stuart's perspective, the shareholders agreement for High Quality Fasteners should address issues such as:

- What if Jim resigns or is dismissed from his employment during the five-year period? If this happens, Stuart would presumably want to ensure that Jim's shares are transferred back. There would then be the question of price – should the shares be sold back at market value or at a discount to market value?

- When Stuart ceases to hold more than 50 per cent of the shares in High Quality Fasteners, he will want to ensure that he retains certain basic rights, such as the right to continue as a director and the right to veto certain important business decisions (for example, the decision to wind up the company or to issue shares to a third party).

- Jim should be bound by restraint-of-trade obligations, so that if he leaves his employment or ceases to be a shareholder he will be prevented from working for a competitor or soliciting customers or employees. From a legal perspective Stuart should bear in mind that these obligations may only be enforceable if he can prove that they are 'reasonable' in all the circumstances. This is a complex area of law that is outside the scope of this book.

From Jim's perspective, the shareholders agreement for High Quality Fasteners should address issues such as:

- how Stuart will transition day-to-day operational control over the five-year period, including the impact on Stuart's salary as his working hours and contribution reduce.

- a clear dividend policy, particularly as Jim may need to fund some or all of the purchase price for Stuart's shares out of dividend income.

- how Jim will be involved in major decisions in the early stages when he is still a minority shareholder.

- restraint-of-trade obligations to bind Stuart once he has completely sold out of the business.

Tony

In progressing the staged succession, *it is crucial for Stuart to bear Tony in mind.*

Although Tony has professed to have no interest in owning or working in the family business, human nature is such that he may in future become jealous of the success that Jim has enjoyed and feel poorly treated by Stuart if the business performs well in future years.

Apart from the very real issues of family disharmony, there is also a risk for Stuart that Tony may make a claim against him or his estate in due course, alleging (for example) that the business was sold to Jim at an undervalue and he should be compensated for this.

The key lesson to be learned is that, when doing a staged succession with family members, you must be rigorous in ensuring that the deal is fair and on commercial terms.

So, Stuart should:

- ensure that the sale price is supported by an independent valuation report.

- ensure that his negotiations with Jim are on a commercial basis. It would assist if each of Stuart and Jim have separate legal and accounting/financial advisers in those negotiations.

- keep an open dialogue with Tony throughout the process and disclose to him as much information as possible.

While a process of this nature will certainly result in additional transaction costs for Stuart, it will give everyone peace of mind and reduce the risk of Tony querying the process or making a claim at some point in the future. And at the end of the day, what price can you put on family harmony?

Asset protection – family law claims

If you have a family business, you may be concerned that the spouse(s) of your children could bring a claim against the business assets upon a marriage breakdown. Or, you may have the same concerns if your own marriage were to fail.

Fears of this nature can sometimes be a spoken or unspoken impediment to a staged succession or other family transition strategy.

With so many marriages ending in divorce, these concerns are certainly legitimate. Nowadays the courts have incredibly broad powers to apportion assets between spouses, and between unmarried partners who were in a live-in relationship, on any basis that they see fit. Particularly if you have a number of children that you would like to see take over the business, what is the likelihood that one of them will get divorced? Statistically speaking, it is scarily high.

A family or private client lawyer may therefore be a valuable part of your business succession planning process. They use tools such as pre-nuptial agreements, estate planning and other asset protection strategies to ensure that your best-laid plans are not jeopardised by known or future marital issues.

I must say that I am constantly amazed by some of the clever strategies that my colleagues who work in this area come up with. None of us like to think that the worst may happen, but if it does it is wonderfully reassuring to know that someone is watching your back.

Is a staged succession right for your business?

The answer to this may depend upon whether your proposed successor is the right person to take your business to the next level.

Too often I have seen business owners either select the wrong person or fail to ensure that the 'right' person is sufficiently trained to take on an ownership role in the business.

Some common mistakes are:

- The mistaken belief that unless an employee is immediately given equity in the business that person will leave. Employees may want to be paid well and valued for their contribution, but it does not necessarily follow that the reward should be equity in your business. There are many other ways to motivate senior staff, such as bonus arrangements, phantom share schemes and other benefits that can be linked to performance and create loyalty without 'giving away the farm'.
- Selling equity to a long-serving employee out of a sense of obligation or moral commitment, where that person does not have the necessary attributes to help take the business forward.
- Selling equity to a large number of employees, and thereby creating an unmanageable shareholder group.
- Giving away equity to an employee rather than selling it. People do not appreciate what they don't have to pay for – it's as simple as that.

Succession story – the McKenzie family

Greg and Pam McKenzie are in their early sixties. Until recently they were the sole owners of a business that imports automotive parts and sells them on.

Their son and daughter, Fraser and Harriet, both work in the business. Fraser became the managing director two years ago and is performing strongly in that role. Harriet is the financial controller and is also a strong performer. Greg and Pam are semi-retired, having already transitioned the management of the business to their children and two other key employees.

Greg and Pam wish to transfer the ownership of the business to their children and are keen that this should be at full value in order to fund their retirement. However, neither Fraser nor Harriet has the capital to acquire the business outright. While they trust their children implicitly, Greg and Pam also wish to protect themselves against one of their children changing their mind and seeking a new career path.

Greg and Pam implemented the following ownership succession plan:

- Each of them sold half of their respective interests in the business to Fraser and Harriet, at full value. With the help of a tax lawyer, they structured the sale in a way that was tax effective.
- Fraser and Harriet will pay for their part of the business over three years. They will fund this primarily out of dividend income. It was therefore necessary to prepare some detailed

financial projections to ensure that there would be sufficient dividends to fund the acquisition.

- To protect their interests, Greg and Pam took security from Fraser and Harriet over the shares that were sold. If Fraser or Harriet do not make the repayments, then Greg and Pam could take back the shares.
- A shareholders agreement was put in place between Greg, Pam, Fraser and Harriet, which (among other things) required that if Fraser or Harriet leave the business within the three-year period, they must sell back their shares at the lower of cost and market value.
- After the third year, the family intends to renegotiate, with a view to Fraser and Harriet (and perhaps the other two key employees) purchasing the balance of Greg and Pam's equity at that time.

Who is the 'right person'?

Before discussing the possibility of selling some equity in your business with your proposed successor, you should go through a process of assessing whether or not that person is appropriate. Otherwise you risk creating an expectation that is not fulfilled, or making a mistake for which you will pay dearly.

This process of review is crucial whether or not the person is an existing employee of the business, and whether or not they are a family member. *Business ownership is the 'jewel in the crown' and should not be given away lightly.*

It is sometimes useful to obtain independent, external help for such a process. It can be hard to have a high degree of objectivity about (particularly) a candidate with whom you have worked for a long time and who may also be a family member.

Some objective criteria that you might consider in determining whether the candidate is the 'right person' are as follows:

1. Does the candidate have the necessary skills not only for their own role (which it is assumed they perform competently) but also to assist in running the business? If not, are they willing and capable of learning these skills? For example, are they financially literate with an understanding of balance sheets, profit and loss accounts and cash flow statements? Do they understand about budgeting and cost control? It is often a significant mental leap for a person to change from an employee mindset to that of a business owner. Training and mentoring may be required.

2. Does the candidate have the ability to assist you in growing the business? A staged succession that results in you ultimately owning a smaller piece of a

much bigger pie makes financial sense. But if the size of the pie will remain the same after selling down your equity, your financial imperative may be less compelling.

3. Is the candidate someone that you can work closely with over the staged succession period? Do they share your goals and aspirations for the business and *have the same values?* Never underestimate these cultural issues.

4. Does the candidate actually want to take this on? If you have a family business, you may have a certain vision or expectation that your son or daughter will take it over one day. However, they may have very different ideas of their own! I have particularly seen this occur in businesses set up by entrepreneurs who 'came from nothing', have little schooling but plenty of commercial acumen, and who build a great business to provide a better life and education for their children. The children take full advantage of these opportunities, and go on to become doctors, lawyers or other professionals. Having become successful in their own area of expertise, the last thing they want to do is take on the business that their parent built. An open and honest dialogue on both sides is therefore extremely important. You need to apply the mirror test to yourself, to ensure that you are not projecting your own dreams and aspirations onto your children.

Setting your children up financially

You don't necessarily need to give your business to your children in order to set them up financially.

This is an obvious statement, but one that you can sometimes overlook when your own identity and sense of value has become intrinsically linked to your business.

I have heard many business owners say things like *'We will never sell; this business is our children's inheritance.'* However, those business owners should reflect on the fact that there are many ways to ensure that future generations are financially secure. It doesn't necessarily involve giving them your business. This is particularly the case if the children are not ready to take on running the business or have other plans or aspirations.

By passing the business on to your children, you may be putting all of their financial eggs 'in one basket'.

In contrast, selling the business and then setting them up with the sale proceeds would allow them to spread their risk by investing in a broader and more diverse portfolio of assets.

KEY LEARNINGS FROM THIS CHAPTER:

- To make a staged succession work, your successor must be the right person to take the business forward. Training and mentoring may be required.

- A shareholders agreement is important to protect you during the period of co-ownership.

- When transitioning the business to family members, do so in a way that is fair and transparent. You will otherwise risk alienating those family members who do not participate.

- You do not need to give your business to your children to set them up financially. There may be better ways to achieve this.

Chapter 6

Going to the market: Trade sale

In this chapter you will learn

tips and traps for taking a business to market

and

how to run a successful sale process

What is a trade sale?

The phrase 'trade sale' means selling your entire business to a third-party buyer.

That buyer may either be a competitor looking to grow their business, or a financial or institutional buyer looking to generate a return on their invested capital.

A trade sale can happen in various different ways. It can occur through a formal process, with you appointing an investment banker or other adviser to take your business to the market. Or it can occur informally – for example, if you are approached by a competitor who wishes to buy your business.

Share sale versus business sale

If you operate your business through a private company, there are basically two ways in which you can structure a trade sale. Either, you can sell the shares in the company, or the company can sell its business and assets.

Or, if your business is operated through a unit trust, similarly you can either sell the units in the trust (broadly equivalent to a share sale), or the trust can sell its business and assets.

As you will read later on, there are many crucial differences between a share (or unit) sale and a business sale. The following example illustrates how these alternatives work.

ABC Plumbing Co Pty Ltd

David and Marika are a husband and wife who each own 50 per cent of the shares in ABC Plumbing Co Pty Ltd ('ABC Plumbing Co'), a successful domestic plumbing company.

Pipe World Limited is a large publicly listed competitor which is on the 'acquisition trail'. Pipe World has recently approached David and Marika and expressed interest in buying them out.

The sale of David and Marika's business to Pipe World could either be structured as a share sale or as a business sale.

Under a share sale transaction, David and Marika would each sell their shares in ABC Plumbing Co to Pipe World. Upon the completion of that sale, Pipe World would therefore own 100 per cent of the shares in ABC Plumbing Co, making ABC Plumbing Co a wholly owned subsidiary of Pipe World.

Under a business sale transaction, ABC Plumbing Co itself would sell its various assets – such as its goodwill, plant and equipment, business name, rights under contracts, and stock in trade – to Pipe World.

Following completion of the business sale, David and Marika would still therefore own their shares in ABC Plumbing Co. ABC Plumbing Co would at that point have no assets, other than the sale price that it received from Pipe World. So, David and Marika would then need to extract the sale price from ABC Plumbing Co, for example by paying themselves a dividend. They would then need to wind up ABC Plumbing Co (which at that point would be an empty 'shell').

The differences between a share sale and business sale

The commercial, legal, taxation and financial effects of a share sale can be very different to those of a business sale.

It is therefore crucial that you have a basic understanding of the key differences, and work with your advisers to determine your preferred structure, before taking your business to market.

In this way, you will be in the driving seat to put forward what suits you best rather than letting the buyer dictate this to you.

Conventional wisdom says that if you are a seller it is better to sell the shares in a company, but if you are a buyer it is better to buy the business and assets. However, this rule of thumb does not always hold true; it is important to assess every transaction on its merits. For example, your company may have valuable tax losses which (subject to complying with various stringent legal requirements) may be possible for the buyer to access if they acquire your shares.

Here are some of the key differences between a share sale and a business sale:

1. If a buyer acquires the shares in your company, they will take on that company lock, stock and barrel as an entity with all of its assets and liabilities. This includes all unknown liabilities or 'skeletons in the closet'.

As a seller, you need to understand that this is a big and scary commitment for a buyer to take on. It means that if, for example, your company provided some negligent advice or did some 'creative' tax planning many years ago, all of these liabilities may come back to bite the buyer.

By contrast, in a business sale transaction the buyer will only acquire your assets and will not generally take on responsibility for creditors or other liabilities.

The fear of skeletons in the closet is the number one reason why the acquisition of shares in a private company – particularly one with a long or chequered history – is generally not appealing to a buyer.

2. A business sale allows the buyer to 'cherry pick' the specific assets that they would like to acquire, without taking on your company as a whole. This is illustrated by the following example.

Fresh Co.

Say that Gina owns 100 per cent of the shares in a food manufacturing company called Fresh Co. That company owns both the operational business assets (such as the machinery in the factory and rights under contracts with supermarkets) and also the land upon which the factory is built. It is a large freehold site, which is worth significantly more than the business. Various trade buyers are interested in acquiring Fresh Co's business, but they do not want to commit the capital that would be required to buy the land. By selling its business and assets, Fresh Co can keep the land and lease it to the buyer following sale. However, if Gina were to sell the shares in Fresh Co to a buyer, she would either need to:

- transfer the land out of Fresh Co first, triggering tax issues and other complexities

OR

- increase the sale price by the value of the land, making Fresh Co unattractive to most buyers.

3. Depending on current tax laws and the availability of any particular relief or concessions, there can sometimes be a tax advantage for you in selling the shares in a company rather than its business and assets. This is because there can be a 'double tax' issue with a business sale, that is:

- the company will generally incur a liability for corporate tax upon the sale of its business and assets; and
- you, the shareholder in the company, will then need to extract the sale proceeds from the company by way of a dividend, capital return or similar. There will then be another amount of tax for you to pay on that dividend or other payment.

This is in contrast to a share sale transaction, where there is only a single amount of tax to pay, being the tax due from you (the shareholder) on the sale of your shares.

4. On a business sale transaction, once the sale has occurred you are left with the 'shell' of the company to wind up (and the associated hassle and expense). This is in contrast to a share sale, where you dispose of the entire company and can therefore exit 'clean'.

5. If a buyer can be persuaded to acquire the shares in your company, they will normally undertake a more rigorous due diligence investigation. For example, tax due diligence would be necessary, as the buyer will be acquiring the company with all of its historical tax characteristics. The buyer will also seek additional warranty and indemnity comfort from you to cover them against unknown liabilities. This is the main 'trade off' for the other benefits of selling your shares rather than the business and assets.

Taking a business to market

So how do you take your business to market? Here is a brief overview:

1. Appoint a professional team

You should never undertake a trade sale process without appropriate professional help. Depending on the size of the transaction, the team will usually comprise a lead adviser, an accountant, a lawyer and a tax adviser.

Further information on selecting and managing your professional team is set out in chapter 10.

2. Obtain a valuation

If you are looking to take your business to the market, one useful tip is to obtain your own valuation first. This will help you to assess any offers that are made and to determine your reserve or 'walk away' price.

Obtaining a valuation is also a useful part of preparing your business for sale, as it should flush out any major issues with the business or the financials. Those issues can then be resolved before you take the business to the market.

Of course, your valuation should be kept confidential and not disclosed to potential buyers.

3. Prepare an Information Memorandum

The Information Memorandum is a marketing document, which contains key information about your business and its assets, liabilities, financial position and prospects. Usually the Information Memorandum will contain some historical financial information, and it may also contain your future financial projections for the business.

You should always take care to ensure that the Information Memorandum contains appropriate disclaimers and does not misrepresent the business. Buyers of failed businesses often point to representations that were made in the Information Memorandum in order bring a damages claim against the seller.

Your lawyer can provide some very useful input on the Information Memorandum in order to reduce these risks. That said, there can sometimes be a fine line between minimising legal risk and weakening the sales pitch. I once amended an Information Memorandum that a client had prepared, to tone down some of the more aggressive representations. At the end of the process my client told me that he knew in advance which sentences I would delete or modify, as these were invariably the parts of which he was most proud from a marketing perspective!

4. Go to the market

Your business can be taken to the market in various ways. These include discretely approaching a select group of potential buyers, advertising, or running a formal tender process. The preferred strategy will depend upon various factors, including the marketability of the business, the extent to which confidentiality is important to you and the number and characteristics of the potential buyers.

Some owners are, quite understandably, concerned about their business being 'shopped around' and their competitors becoming aware that they might be up for sale. If you share this concern, it is crucial for you to work with advisers who understand this and who will be extremely discrete in how they approach potential buyers.

5. Assess indicative offers

Once you have taken the business to the market, you will receive and assess indicative offers from potential buyers. At this stage, you would perhaps also negotiate the terms of those offers on a 'subject to due diligence' basis.

6. Due diligence

The next stage is to provide detailed information about the business to one or more potential buyers who have made an indicative offer. You would generally establish a data room containing all necessary information (such as financials, board meeting minutes, compliance records, key contracts, employee information, customer information and documents of title to key assets). Data rooms are best established via a secure online portal (as opposed to being a physical room).

If there is some highly confidential or commercially sensitive information that you are concerned about providing to potential buyers, you may choose to exclude that information from the data room during the early stages of due diligence. That information would then be disclosed later on, when you have more certainty that the transaction is going to proceed. If you take this approach, it is important that you make the potential buyer(s) aware of the type of information that has been excluded from the data room and let them know at which stage in the process you intend to disclose it.

7. Sale agreement

Once the potential buyer(s) have done their due diligence, it is time to draft, negotiate and execute the sale agreement and any other necessary transaction documents.

8. Completion

The final step comprises payment of the money and transfer of the business to the new owner.

Minimising risk on the sale of your business

From a liability perspective, selling your business can be extremely risky. *Indeed, it may create the most significant risk of legal liability of your business life.* An investment banker friend of mine once described selling your business as 'a licence to get sued'!

Quite understandably, buyers will seek legal comfort from you that the business they are buying is as they expect it to be, based on the information that you have provided (in terms of its financial position, customers, assets, liabilities, profits and prospects). This comfort is obtained through you providing warranties and indemnities in relation to the business. If your business does not perform as expected following the sale, or if there are any hidden liabilities that the buyer later discovers, then the buyer will seek recourse by looking to sue you under those warranties and indemnities.

Buyers who pay top dollar for a business will invariably seek the maximum warranty protection from you. Or conversely, if you want to give no warranties, you should expect nothing more than a 'fire sale' price. *So get realistic – there is a link between the money that you receive and the protection that you give to the buyer.*

Here's an example of how warranties work. Say you are selling the shares in a privately-owned company. In the sale agreement, you give a warranty to the buyer that there are no litigation claims against that company. If the buyer pays you (say) $3 million for the company, but later discovers that there is actually an uninsured product liability claim against the company for $1 million, then effectively the buyer should have only paid you $2 million to reflect this exposure. So, the buyer would bring a warranty claim against you for $1 million.

The schedule of warranties in a sale agreement can run to many pages. *Do not be put off by this.* Clients of mine have sometimes nearly fallen off their chair when faced with ten, twenty, or even thirty pages of warranties as drafted by the buyer's lawyer. However, you should bear in mind that it is generally the technical wording of the warranties, rather than their volume, that determines the amount of legal firepower that the buyer will have against you.

An important part of your lawyer's role is to assist you in sufficiently containing your liability under the warranties and indemnities. When selecting a lawyer, it is crucial that you choose one with experience in these types of transactions and who knows what points to cover to ensure that you are protected.

Some of the key protections that you and your lawyer may seek are:

- ***A right to make disclosures against the warranties.*** This means that the sale agreement will state that the buyer is not allowed to bring a warranty claim against you in respect of any information that was disclosed by you in due diligence. So, using the above example, as long as you disclosed the $1 million product liability claim before the sale agreement is signed, the buyer would not be entitled to seek compensation from you in respect of that claim. This is because they are buying with full knowledge of it. Having negotiated a right to make disclosures against the warranties, you must then be rigorous in ensuring that you disclose everything that is relevant. As part of that process, you should never cover up, hide or 'play down' any adverse matters in relation to the business.

- ***A maximum liability cap.*** This means that the sale agreement will state that your maximum liability under the warranties is limited to, say, the total amount of the sale price (or some lower amount).

- ***A 'de minimis' claims threshold.*** This means that the sale agreement will state that the buyer may not bring a warranty claim against you unless the amount of that claim exceeds a certain minimum amount (for example, $50,000). As a general rule, the 'de minimis' claims threshold is usually between one and two per cent of the total amount of the sale price.

- ***A time limit within which a warranty claim may be brought.*** Typically, the warranty claims period is somewhere between 12 months and three years. Sometimes a longer period is negotiated in relation to warranties relating to taxation matters.

Security for warranty claims

A key concern for the buyer will be to ensure that, if they ever need to make a warranty claim, there is some money available to cover that claim. Buyers therefore look for security for your obligations under the warranties. Some examples of such security are:

- a personal guarantee
- a retention from the purchase price. For example, the buyer may seek to place 10 per cent of the purchase price into a bank account controlled by a third-party trustee, to be released to you after two years if no warranty claims have been made
- an earn-out arrangement under which part of the purchase price remains unpaid at completion, to be paid at a later date subject to performance and offset, if necessary, against warranty claims
- a bank guarantee
- a guarantee from other companies that you own
- a mortgage over your real property or other assets.

An important part of the sale negotiation often revolves around the nature and extent of the security to be provided by you to the buyer. This will depend on the specific circumstances of each transaction.

It may be useful for you to discuss this issue with your advisory team before the sale process commences, so you can work out a reasonable security package to offer should the need arise.

Restraint of trade

As I mentioned earlier, the buyer will expect you to enter into restraint-of-trade obligations in the sale agreement. These are obligations not to compete with the business, or to solicit the customers or employees of the business, for a certain period of time following completion. *After all, why would the buyer pay good money for your business if you could set up again in competition again the next day?*

Generally speaking, a restraint-of-trade clause is only enforceable if the buyer can prove that the clause is 'reasonable' in all the circumstances. This means that the legal wording of these clauses can be quite long and detailed in order to maximise the prospects of enforceability. Don't be put off by this.

There can often be a negotiation around the duration and geographical extent of the restraint-of-trade clauses. Unless any special circumstances exist to justify this, it is generally unwise to seek significant 'get outs' from your restraint obligations. This can cause great concern to a buyer, who may think that the reason you are seeking these exceptions is that you have a sinister hidden agenda.

Understanding the tactics of a buyer

Before offering your business for sale, it is important to understand how potential buyers may approach the transaction. Once you understand the mindset of a buyer, it is easier to pre-empt some of the tactics that they may employ.

The manner in which a business is taken to market, and in which the sale and purchase price and terms are negotiated, can be extremely tactical. Like in a game of chess, the trick is to be one step ahead of your 'opponent' and pre-empt their next move.

A typical approach by a buyer might be as follows:

1. Wait until the business is advertised for sale.

2. Put in an attractive offer that is expressed to be non-binding and 'subject to due diligence'.

3. Obtain a period of negotiating exclusivity. In other words, have you agree to a period of (say) three months during which the buyer will have the exclusive right to conduct due diligence and negotiate the detailed terms of the sale without competition from other prospective buyers.

4. During the due diligence investigation, identify as many features of the business as possible that are risky, or which attack the historical or projected earnings of the business, or the credibility of other information that you have provided.

5. As a result of the due diligence investigation, withdraw the original (attractive) offer and substitute a much less attractive offer.

6. Put pressure on you to accept the less attractive offer. The buyer may have additional leverage at this time, because your business has now been 'shopped around' and if it is not sold the prospects of a future sale may be reduced.

Succession story – Beatrice and Holly

Sisters Beatrice and Holly owned and operated a successful specialist recruitment business, which had originally been established by their father.

Holly was the CEO and Beatrice was a senior recruitment consultant. Both in their early fifties, they did not wish to retire but were looking for additional challenges in their careers. They also wanted to diversify their respective assets, as their entire wealth was tied up in the business.

Without a natural successor working in the business, they approached a reputable corporate finance accountant to find a buyer. After a rigorous screening process, their accountant introduced them to another recruitment firm that was looking to expand.

A deal was done whereby:

- Holly would become the manager of the buyer's broader business (giving her the new challenge that she craved).

- Beatrice would continue as a senior recruitment consultant, but would change her focus to mentoring and training the younger recruitment consultants in the buyer's business.

The buyer would pay a significant upfront sum for the business, plus some additional amounts over three years, based on performance in each of those years.

While an 'earn out' arrangement of this nature does not suit everyone, Beatrice and Holly were attracted to it because they were able to take some money off the table upfront and then back themselves to grow the business and maximise their return. Also, due to Holly's ongoing role, they were comfortable that she had the ability to make decisions and control expenditure in order to ensure that earnings were maximised.

To protect their ability to drive the business and maximise earnings in the earn-out period, Beatrice and Holly negotiated various protections in the sale documentation, including:

> - robust employment agreements that enshrined their right to continue in their executive roles during the earn-out period.
> - clear parameters for Holly's CEO role, which gave her the power and autonomy to run the business in a manner that would maximise earnings in the three-year period.
>
> Beatrice and Holly were then able to use the sale proceeds to pay off their mortgages and invest in a broad portfolio of assets. They also used some of the money to assist their adult children to buy homes.

Countering the buyer's tactics

Some of counter-tactics that you could employ against the approach outlined above may be as follows:

Buyer's tactic 1: Wait until the business is advertised for sale.

Your counter-tactic: Rather than relying solely on advertising to unknown third parties as part of a sale process, ensure that you identify and develop relationships with potential buyers at an early stage. Ensure that the brand awareness and visibility of your business is high. In this way, you will maximise the chances of potential buyers approaching you (rather than you approaching them).

When a buyer approaches you, you will be in the 'driving seat' and have greater leverage in the negotiations. Equally important is ensuring that you are always in a position to present a saleable business to potential buyers in case an approach is made. This brings us back to the key principles of prior planning and running the business from day one with succession in mind.

Buyer's tactic 2: Put in an attractive offer that is expressed to be non-binding and 'subject to due diligence'.

Your counter-tactic: It is difficult to overcome the buyer's offer being conditional upon due diligence. However, some ways for you to at least test whether the potential buyer is genuine in making their offer are:

- Obtain a deposit from the buyer upfront. It may also be possible to negotiate for a small portion of that deposit to be non-refundable if the transaction does not proceed.
- Be careful what information you provide in the due diligence phase. If the potential buyer is a competitor, perhaps you should withhold highly confidential information until a formal, binding offer has been made. In any event, you will need a robust confidentiality agreement to be signed by the potential buyer before due diligence commences.

Buyer's tactic 3: *Obtain a period of negotiating exclusivity.*

Your counter-tactic: Consider whether a tender process can be run, whereby a select number of appropriately qualified bidders are simultaneously given the opportunity to conduct due diligence on your business. In this way, competitive tension may be created. From working with buyers, I understand how keenly this competitive tension can be felt. Rather than putting in a 'low ball' offer to sound you out, a serious buyer will be much more likely to make a decent bid if they are participating in a competitive process.

Or at least try to limit the exclusivity period to as short a time frame as possible, to put pressure on the buyer to ensure that they progress their due diligence investigations in a timely manner. You may also ask them to commit to a clear and prescriptive due diligence process which contains 'milestones' that must be achieved along the way if their exclusivity is to be preserved.

Buyer's tactic 4: *During due diligence, identify as many features of the business as possible that are risky, cannot be supported or which attack the historical or projected earnings of the business or the credibility of the owner.*

Your counter-tactic: Ensure that you are absolutely rigorous in preparing due diligence information for provision to potential buyers. That information must be complete, accurate and current. Identify any 'sticky' issues early in the process and address them in a way that shows them in the most positive light (without being misleading).

*I really want to emphasise to you the need to be **extremely well prepared** for the due diligence phase.*

If you provide a data room which is incomplete or hurriedly thrown together, or if you are unable to respond quickly to the buyer's information requests, you will quickly lose control of the process and credibility with the buyer. I have seen this happen many times and it is just embarrassing. You are asked some questions about your business and then spend the next few days desperately 'scratching around' trying to find the answers. The buyer will think that if you are this incompetent now, how efficiently have you really run your business over the years? Or, even worse, the buyer may think that you have something to hide.

Buyer's tactic 5: *As a result of the due diligence investigation, withdraw the original (attractive) offer and substitute a much less attractive offer.*

Your counter-tactic: Your approach in steps 1 to 4 will drastically reduce the risk of this happening significantly. And if it does occur, you should hopefully have some options as you will at least be well prepared to quickly commence a sale process with alternative buyers.

Tips and traps for the unwary

Selling your business usually happens only once or twice in a lifetime. When going through the process, it can feel like being in a pressure cooker of emotion and stress. And whilst in this highly-charged environment, you are still expected to act calm, keep your head, and make various important decisions and judgment calls along the way.

Here are some of the common mistakes that are made by business owners when offering their business for sale:

Overselling or misrepresenting the business

Business owners are often good salespeople. In their ardour to sell their business for the best price, they can sometimes 'cross the line' into misrepresentation.

If you misrepresent the assets, liabilities, profitability or prospects of your business, you will risk a legal claim by the buyer. In certain circumstances the buyer may even argue that they are entitled to walk away from the transaction altogether, because the sale agreement has been *made void by your misrepresentation.*

Importantly, you should be aware of the following:

- Any Information Memorandum or other offer document in relation to your business should be carefully reviewed to ensure that it is true, accurate and not misleading.

- One key risk area is the provision of financial projections to the buyer (i.e. forecasts of how the business will perform in the future). As I mentioned earlier in this book, the provision of credible financial projections can be a powerful way to sell your business for the best price. But, if you provide misleading projections you will find yourself on the wrong end of a writ. Take steps to reduce the risk by ensuring that your projections are conservative, prepared on a reasonable basis, and not based upon mere hypothetical assumptions. *It is crucial that you get your accountant to help you with this.* You should then make it clear to the buyer that no warranties or guarantees will be given that the business will perform in accordance with your projections.

- A misrepresentation is not always something that is actually said to the buyer. Misrepresentation can also occur through silence or omission. For example, a prospective buyer asks you a number of detailed questions about known product liability claims against the business. You answer all of these questions truthfully, but do not disclose that yesterday a new, potentially significant product liability claim was threatened by a customer over the telephone. If a formal claim is then brought by that customer after the business is sold, then the buyer may allege misrepresentation based upon your silence in failing to disclose the new product liability claim.

Looking for a 'zero risk' position

This chapter has looked at some of the legal risks that are associated with a trade sale process – particularly the risk of claims for breach of warranties in the sale agreement. Because of the risks involved, the sale process generally requires heavy legal support for both the buyer and the seller.

In this environment, you can sometimes become nervous and concerned about legal risk to a degree that is counter-productive. This concern may be exacerbated if your advisers are over-zealous, or if they are not familiar with corporate transactions and therefore take an overly conservative approach.

As with any business decision, you can never realistically expect to achieve a 'zero risk' position. This is particularly the case if you are looking to sell for the highest price. Like ying and yang, risk and reward go together.

In order to complete a sale transaction that works for both parties, you should expect to:

- give some reasonable warranties and indemnities in relation to the business and its financial and trading position
- provide reasonable security for claims against those warranties and indemnities
- give a robust obligation to the buyer not to compete with the business or solicit customers or employees for a reasonable period of time following the sale.

The sale agreement is all about sharing and apportioning risk appropriately between yourself and the buyer. The most important thing is to ensure that you clearly understand the level of risk that you are taking on, and that this is something that you can live with when weighed up against the amount of money that the buyer is paying you.

At the end of the day, ensuring that the buyer has no nasty surprises once they have bought your business is the very best protection you can get. ***Remember the mantra of disclosure, disclosure and more disclosure!***

KEY LEARNINGS FROM THIS CHAPTER:

- Obtain advice upfront on the preferred structure for your transaction – should it be a share sale (or unit sale if you run your business through a unit trust) or a business sale?

- Consider obtaining a valuation before you take your business to market, to assist with determining your reserve or 'walk away' price.

- Beware of misrepresenting your business through the information memorandum, your discussions with the buyer, or what you omit to tell the buyer.

- Expect to give some reasonable warranties and a robust restraint of trade obligation.

- Ensure that you negotiate appropriate limitations of liability. However, do not expect to achieve a 'zero risk' position.

- Always undertake a rigorous process of disclosing all relevant information to the buyer – including the 'bad stuff'.

Chapter 7

Sophisticated investors: the role of private equity

In this chapter you will learn

how private equity can assist with your exit strategy

and

the key features of a private equity transaction

The venture capital and private equity industry

The growth of the venture capital and private equity industry has significantly changed the face of private and family-owned business succession.

Unfortunately, this industry has sometimes been unfairly tarnished by its detractors, through allegations of greed and unscrupulous conduct. The stereotype is that private equity and venture capital funds look to buy businesses for as low a price as possible, strip out the overheads, and then sell them high as quickly as possible with little regard to non-financial issues.

Critics of the industry have used colourful phrases such as 'vulture capital', 'pirate equity', or 'pump and dump' to describe this approach.

But this cynical view of the industry is dangerous, as it can close your mind to the very real opportunities to grow your business and realise significant value with the assistance of private equity.

My personal experience of the venture capital and private equity industry has been extremely positive. Many of my clients have become millionaires through partnering with these investors to grow and sell their businesses. The best private equity funds also add significant value along the way, through their knowledge and experience in operating and growing companies.

For these reasons, I am keen to explain how private equity investors can help you to achieve a successful exit through:

- a management buy-out or buy-in, or
- provision of expansion capital to grow your business before sale.

So, how does it all work?

The private equity business model

Private equity funds are investment funds which acquire shareholdings in unlisted companies. The ones which invest in start-up or early stage businesses are generally called venture capital funds.

The investors in private equity funds are typically large institutional funds, which are looking to expose a small part of their portfolio to the unlisted market.

The typical private equity investment cycle works as follows:

- Identify a business that falls within the fund's investment criteria. Private equity funds are normally attracted to businesses which have positive earnings and a compelling growth story.

- Identify whether the current management team are the best people to take the business to the next level. If so, invite them to co-invest in the business (this is known as a management buy-out or 'MBO'). If not, find an external management team to co-invest (this is known as a management buy-in or 'MBI'). And believe it or not, transactions involving both members of the existing management team and some external candidates are sometimes called a buy-in / management buy-out or BIMBO!

- Identify a growth strategy for the business. Examine the business, the market and the management team to assess the likelihood of that strategy being successful.

- Purchase the business using money from the fund together with bank debt and (often relatively small) contributions from the management buy-out or buy-in team.

- Grow the business over a three-to-five-year period. The growth may be organic or may be achieved by acquiring other businesses to 'bolt on' to the original investment.

- During the three-to-five-year period, limit distributions to shareholders and instead use the profits of the business to pay down the bank debt.

- Sell or float the business at the end of the three-to-five-year period, hopefully for a substantial profit.

Private equity funds can assist with your exit strategy

One way in which private equity funds can assist with your exit strategy is to provide the financial firepower and other support that is required for your management team to acquire the business.

Or, they can provide expansion capital to enable your business to make acquisitions or establish new business lines. In this scenario you would remain a meaningful shareholder in the business, but your ownership interest would be diluted. You would then work with the private equity investor as co-owners over the next few years to grow the business, and then exit together via a trade sale or initial public offer on the stock exchange (IPO).

Some of the positive features of dealing with a private equity investor are:

- Selling to a management buy-out team with private equity backing has some of the same desirable features as a staged succession (see Chapter 5). The transition of the business is likely to be smooth because the same people will be running it on a day-to-day basis. However, unlike the staged succession where you are paid 'on the drip feed' over time, if you sell to a private equity fund you are likely to receive most or all of the sale price upfront.

- Because management buy-out teams have an intimate knowledge of your business, you would generally not need to give them the same level of warranties and indemnities on sale as you would to a third party buyer.

- Private equity buyers are experienced in growing and grooming companies for sale. So, they can often add significant value for the benefit of all upon exit. Private equity executives are generally very bright, energetic and well-qualified people who can bring great skills to your business such as financial modelling and analysis, finding and assessing acquisition targets, and managing growth.

Succession story – Ashwin

In his early thirties, Ashwin established a retail fashion business. After ten years and a lot of hard work, the business had grown into a substantial enterprise with outlets nation-wide.

Ashwin was becoming increasingly jaded by his long working hours and constant travel to each of the company's stores. His family life had also suffered. Ashwin wanted to spend more time with his children while they were still at school, and to pursue his other interest – property development.

At the same time, the business continued to grow. Indeed, the business had significant 'untapped' opportunities to increase market share by buying various competitors who were well known to Ashwin.

Ashwin put in place the following succession plan:

- Ashwin's accountant introduced him to a private equity fund which had a good understanding of the retail sector. That fund purchased 50 per cent of Ashwin's business, and also injected additional equity capital to assist with acquiring the competitors that Ashwin had identified as targets. This diluted Ashwin's shareholding down to 30 per cent in total.

- The key terms of the transaction were as follows:

  o Ashwin would relinquish his role as CEO after a twelve-month handover period.

  o Ashwin would continue to consult to the business on a part-time basis. His role would be to identify potential acquisition targets and assist in the negotiation of those acquisitions.

> ○ The parties would continue to grow the business over the following three years, and then look to exit via a trade sale or floating the company on a stock exchange.
>
> Two years have now passed, and one of the target acquisitions has completed. This has added significant revenue and profitability to the group. Ashwin has not slowed down as much as he had anticipated, but certainly has a more balanced life with less travel.
>
> The private equity fund has assisted Ashwin through 'corporatising' the business, bringing in disciplines such as monthly board meetings and timely financial reporting.
>
> While he now owns only 30 per cent of the business, Ashwin is confident that when it is ultimately sold or floated he will make significantly more than what he received for the original 50 per cent.

Tips and traps when dealing with a private equity investor

Before entering into a transaction with a private equity investor, you should be aware of the following:

1. Private equity fund managers make their money from buying and selling businesses. Their funds also generally prescribe a finite time period within which monies must be returned to the investors. If the horizon for your exit from the business is greater than three to five years, then an ongoing co-investment with private equity may not be for you.

2. If you are to be a co-owner of the business along with a private equity investor for a period of time, the cultural fit between yourself and that investor is extremely important. I have seen the relationship with private equity investors sour when there has not been sufficient discussion upfront about each party's expectations.

Here are some issues that you should discuss with the private equity fund before entering into a long-term co-investment:

- Do they have a 'hands on' style and like to get intimately involved in management decisions? Or, do they prefer to let you get on with things with minimal input? Either of these styles may suit certain businesses and not others.
- What is their expectation as to timing for exit?
- To what extent will decision-making authority be delegated to the board or yourself personally? Which decisions will be reserved for the private equity fund?
- How many board representatives will they require?

- Have they previously replaced management teams, and if so how many times and for what reasons?
- How will your shareholding be affected if they inject additional funding for growth down the track?
- What incentives do they offer for exceptional growth (for example, would some additional shares or other bonuses be given)?

If you are selling down part of your business to a private equity investor, you should prepare to be 'corporatised'. One valuable aspect of introducing a private equity investor is that they will ensure that the business adopts a governance model that will allow it to take the next step in its growth cycle and eventually become ready for trade sale or IPO. So, you should expect that the private equity investor will take steps such as introducing regular board and shareholders meetings (and ensuring that those meetings are appropriately minuted), improving financial reporting systems, and ensuring that there is some independent or non-executive representation on the board. *This can sometimes come as a shock to entrepreneurial people who have run the business their own way for many years.*

Private equity investors are extremely sophisticated buyers of businesses. They buy and sell businesses for a living and surround themselves with the best advisers. So, you should always :

- ensure that your business is well prepared before approaching them
- expect them to conduct a rigorous due diligence investigation and negotiate hard

- obtain good professional advice early, in order to enhance your position in attracting and negotiating with them. Approaching them through a corporate adviser can provide additional credibility, and may mean that you are more likely to be taken seriously

- present an honest, 'warts and all' picture. If you try to pull the wool over their eyes, they will find out!

KEY LEARNINGS FROM THIS CHAPTER:

- Be alive to the opportunities that exist through private equity funding. Private equity can help fund your management team to buy the business, or provide expansion capital to help you grow before exiting.

- Private equity investors can add significant value through 'corporatising' your business to prepare it for IPO or trade sale.

- Private equity investors are extremely sophisticated buyers of businesses. Be very well prepared before you deal with them. Approaching them through a corporate adviser may increase your credibility.

Chapter 8

Going public: listing on a stock exchange

In this chapter you will learn

IPO processes

and

whether an IPO is right for your business

The IPO

An initial public offer ('IPO') is the first sale of shares in a company to the public. The IPO is achieved through that company listing on a stock exchange.

If you are a small business owner, I am conscious that an IPO is unlikely to be on your radar. That said, I still feel that it is important to mention IPOs for a few different reasons:

- For those who do have a sizeable business, an IPO can be a very exciting and remunerative exit option
- Some of the lessons about grooming your business for IPO are universal and can assist any business owner
- Even if you start off small, remember that an IPO can be the culmination of various other preliminary strategies. For example, you might start off with a tiny business which you look to grow through acquisition (see Chapter 2). You might then sell part of that business to the management team (see Chapter 5) or seek a private equity investor to 'ramp up' your growth strategy (see Chapter 7). Then, a few years down the track, your endeavours may culminate in an IPO.

Benefits of an IPO

When considering your exit options, bear in mind that *some of the largest multiples in history have been achieved by business owners undertaking a successful IPO.*

And if that isn't enough to whet your appetite, the other benefits of an IPO can include:

- the ability to sell part of your stake in the business upon IPO, but retain an ongoing interest
- liquidity – a ready market to sell shares at a time that suits you (subject to corporate governance requirements and insider trading rules)
- the opportunity to return to the market on subsequent occasions, to raise funds for future growth or other purposes
- a transparent valuation methodology for your shares – their value is determined by the market
- flexibility to acquire other businesses through offering shares (often called

'scrip consideration') to the owner(s), or a mixture of cash and scrip consideration
- the ability to increase your business profile and make your business and brand famous
- the ability to attract and reward key personnel with equity in the business, through employee share and option plans.

Transition

It is important to understand that you are unlikely to realise 100 per cent of your interest in the business immediately upon IPO.

In order to sell the IPO effectively to potential investors, it is normally necessary for you to retain a substantial interest in the business ongoing. The marketing rationale behind this is sound – if you are not personally prepared to back the business going forward, how can you hope to persuade others to do so?

Realisation of the full value of your interest in the business is therefore likely to be a gradual process, to be achieved through selling down in a structured way in the public environment in the years following the IPO.

Similarly, it is also unlikely that you will be able to retire from your executive role in the business upon (or immediately following) IPO. Investors in the IPO will be backing the current management team, and will want some comfort that you and others will stick around to drive the business in the months and years following IPO.

If you are considering an IPO, it is therefore important that you view this as a 'transition' for your business, rather than an immediate exit strategy. It is not a 'big bang' or instantaneous result like some trade sales.

For this reason, it is also important for you to recognise that the share price in the years *following the IPO* will probably be more important to you personally than the share price *upon IPO*. So, rather than being focussed on maximising the share price upon IPO, the smart approach may actually be to have a more modest IPO price which is attractive to investors. This should create a core group of loyal investors who will profit from the IPO and continue to support the business in future. In turn, this will assist you in selling down and realising the full value of your investment in the years following the IPO.

Is an IPO right for my business?

Whether or not an IPO is right for your business will depend on a number of factors, including the market dynamics and sentiment at the time, the size of your business, your future growth aspirations, and whether the business is sufficiently 'corporatised' to survive in the listed environment.

One aspect that business owners sometimes overlook when considering an IPO is the relentless growth expectation of the public markets. Mature, stable, small to medium-sized businesses do not generally create much excitement upon IPO. A high growth profile is a pre-requisite.

In order to be a good candidate for an IPO, your business must also have a certain size and critical mass, because the compliance costs associated with operating a listed company may otherwise outweigh the benefits.

Indeed, it is arguable that many companies which are currently listed should actually not be listed at all. These are often relatively small companies with one or two major shareholders and whose shares are not significantly traded (unless in the hands of day traders). They are saddled with a significant compliance burden, and do not obtain the key benefit of liquidity.

The IPO process

The IPO process involves a number of key procedural steps. As a brief overview, these steps are generally as follows:

- Generally, your company must satisfy various criteria before it can be listed, including minimum levels of assets, profitability, and 'spread', i.e. a certain minimum number of shareholders is required before the company can be admitted to the official list.

- Corporate restructure. For various reasons, including asset protection and minimising legal liability in connection with the IPO, it may be necessary to restructure your business to ensure that it is in an appropriate legal form to be floated.

- Structuring and marketing the offer. Assistance will be required from a stockbroker to structure the offer and sell it to key investors. The stockbroker may also underwrite the offer. Underwriting fees are significant, but are usually paid out of the IPO proceeds.

- Prospectus preparation and due diligence. This is a detailed process involving a 'due diligence committee' comprised of members of the board and senior management of the business, the lawyer to the offer, the corporate or financial adviser, the underwriter, and the accountant. In order to minimise the liability of the company's directors and others, a rigorous process must be undertaken whereby each statement in the prospectus is verified against source documents. Verification is well known in the corporate advisory world as an important but extremely lengthy and tedious process. I certainly spent many long hours on this task as a young lawyer, and carry the emotional scars to this day! I remember on one transaction the verification documents were so voluminous that I needed to *hire a van* to transport them to the final meeting!

- Professional reports. Often, various professional reports are included in the prospectus, such as an accountant's report or a particular industry-specific report. For example, an IPO of a technology business might include reports from independent specialists which verify the technology.

As you can see, an IPO is a major project. If you undertake one, you should expect that it will consume your life for a period of two to six months. Business owners generally underestimate the time that is necessary to prepare and conduct due diligence and verification on the prospectus, and to 'roadshow' the offer to institutional investors.

Private information becomes public

A key aspect of floating on a stock exchange is the fact that all of the financial and other affairs of the company will cease to be your private information and will be disclosed in the public arena. *This is an aspect that the owners of a private or family business can sometimes struggle with.*

The law generally requires the prospectus to contain all information that is material for a potential investor to know about the business. This, of course, includes all of the 'bad stuff' that you would not otherwise trumpet to the marketplace. The extent to which information must be disclosed in the IPO process often comes as a surprise.

Following the IPO, continuous disclosure obligations will apply to oblige your newly-listed company to promptly disclose all price sensitive information to the market (with certain limited exceptions).

If you are a private person and are uncomfortable with the level of disclosure required in the public forum, an IPO may not be an appropriate exit strategy for you. I recall this once dawning on some clients of mine as we went through the early stages of prospectus drafting. My clients were deeply private people who had never 'flashed their money around'. They found it disturbing to consider disclosing so many things to the market that were closely guarded secrets, to the extent that they abandoned the IPO process and ultimately progressed another confidential exit strategy.

Pre-IPO steps

If your ultimate goal is to IPO, you ideally need to plan for this some years in advance, to ensure that you have appropriate systems and governance in place to cope with the listed environment. This can be a big step for private businesses, which is often underestimated.

The necessary changes reflect some of the aspects that we have considered in Chapters 3 and 4. In particular, they include:

- ensuring that you have a functional board and governance structure in place, with regular meetings and a proper flow of financial and other information to the board. The board might also include some independent, non-executive directors
- ensuring that there is a clear separation of your business assets and non-business assets
- unwinding or varying contracts or other arrangements between the business and you or your family members which are not on strict arm's length terms
- ensuring that annual accounts are prepared and audited by a credible accounting firm.

As indicated in Chapter 7, a private equity investment in your business can sometimes be a useful stepping-stone from private ownership into the listed environment.

Prior to the IPO, you should take time to communicate effectively with employees and explain the reasons for the IPO and the effect it will have on the business. You may also choose to motivate staff with employee share offers and the like, which can increase their 'buy in' and excitement about the IPO. Careful consideration of the taxation treatment of employee share plans is required before they are implemented.

Succession story — Michael

Michael and his children ran a successful third-generation family business, manufacturing fruit juices and other beverages.

The business had always had reputable products and strong sales, but low brand awareness. The business also had a loyal and long-serving workforce, who were made to feel part of the family team.

In his late fifties, Michael had no immediate plans to slow down or stop work. However, he could foresee this occurring in the next five years or so.

Over the years, Michael had invested significantly into the business, but the need for capital was still pressing. He had big plans to upgrade and extend the factory, and also to purchase another business which would give him the economies of scale necessary to compete effectively against larger players. At this stage of his life, Michael was reluctant to gear up the business with significant new debt, or to liquidate any more of his personal assets to support the business.

With the assistance of a corporate adviser, Michael listed the business on a major stock exchange. The lead-up to the IPO provided him with a wonderful opportunity to create brand awareness in relation to the business, and he did this effectively through a television and newspaper advertising campaign. Suddenly, his brand was being talked about all over the country.

Thanks to the IPO, Michael was able to sell down some of his interest in the business and invest in other assets. At the same time, he maintained a meaningful stake in the business, which also raised enough capital to fuel his growth aspirations.

Over 40 per cent of the staff, at all levels in the business, took up shares in the IPO. This created a 'culture of ownership' that gave the business a strong platform for growth and improvement. The staff gave very positive feedback that they felt part of the vision and financial performance of the business going forward.

The post-IPO world

A common concern of business owners who are considering an IPO is that there may be significant cultural changes following the listing, and that this may worry employees and customers. In reality, such changes are often not as great as they fear.

If managed well, the increased visibility that results from being a listed company can create significant advantages for your business. It can create opportunities with customers, suppliers, potential employees, investors and acquisition targets, who may not otherwise have been aware of your business or its successes.

Some hints and tips for the post-IPO world are as follows:

- Employees are likely to give close (perhaps daily) attention to the share price following IPO. A fall in the share price may cause them concern, even if this is just due to the vagaries of the market. You should be aware of this as part of your ongoing communication strategy with employees.

- A listed company understandably comes under greater scrutiny from shareholders and the media. Accordingly, it is normally useful to have an effective PR strategy both leading up to, and following, the IPO. The IPO is normally a good time to engage a PR consultant, if your business does not already have one.

- It is important to recognise the amount of ongoing senior management time that can be absorbed by dealing with 'capital markets issues', such as briefing investors or considering continuous disclosure announcements. This time commitment can sometimes create a distraction from the day-to-day operation of your business.

- Many business owners hold the mistaken belief that liquidity for their shares will be 'automatic' in the post-IPO world. However, and particularly for smaller listed companies, the reality is often somewhat different. Indeed, you may soak up all the demand for the shares at IPO, leaving little interest from investors following the IPO. A good stockbroker can greatly assist in the crucial first 12 months following IPO, by continuing to promote the business and building up liquidity.

KEY LEARNINGS FROM THIS CHAPTER:

- Many successful exit strategies have culminated in an IPO. However, it is important that you see the IPO as a transition phase rather than an opportunity to 'cash out' one hundred percent on day 1.

- An IPO is appropriate only for businesses which are sufficiently 'corporatised' and which have a compelling growth story.

- Your business needs to be of a certain size and critical mass before it is a good candidate for an IPO. Otherwise, the compliance costs may outweigh the benefits.

- Upon IPO, your private business information will become public.

- Following the IPO, dealing with capital markets issues may soak up a reasonable amount of your time.

Chapter 9

We're in this together: Co-owned businesses and unplanned succession

In this chapter you will learn

how unexpected events may jeopardise your exit strategy

and

how to reduce the risks relating to an unplanned succession

Unplanned succession

The previous chapters looked at how to achieve a planned, orderly sale of your business – for example, through a trade sale, staged succession or IPO. But if you co-own a business, you should also be aware of the possibility of unplanned ownership succession.

An unplanned ownership succession issue may arise if you or any of your business partners:

- die, suffer a serious illness, or become totally and permanently disabled
- resign from an executive role in the business to progress other interests or retire
- cease to perform strongly in an executive role, and need to be removed from the business.

Events of this nature are common in private or family-owned businesses. *And the likelihood increases the more business partners you have and the older they become.*

Whatever your ultimate exit strategy, it pays to prepare for the possibility of an unplanned succession. The main way to do this is through a shareholders agreement. This is an agreement between the shareholders of a private company which regulates their relationship. Shareholders agreements typically deal with matters such as:

- exit mechanisms (both for individual shareholders and for the entire business)
- board and shareholders meetings
- restraint-of-trade obligations
- dividend policy
- issuing new shares and ongoing funding requirements

Depending on how your business is structured, other documents that may perform a similar function to a shareholders agreement include a partnership agreement (if your business is structured as a partnership) or a unitholders agreement (if your business is structured as a unit trust). Also, a short form shareholders agreement which just deals with unplanned exit mechanisms is sometimes called a 'buy/sell agreement'.

In any given year, it is sad but true that the number of clients who engage my law firm to assist with a dispute with their co-owners is always far greater than the number who engage us to prepare a shareholders agreement to protect them in the first place. *And guess what? It costs those clients much more for us fix up their problems in court than it would have done to protect them upfront.*

Some ways in which a shareholders agreement can assist you with unplanned succession, and in which not having one can cause you a major headache, are illustrated by the case studies below.

The first case study examines what can happen upon the death of a co-owner:

SJ Construction

Sarah and Juan are shareholders in a residential building company called SJ Construction. Sarah holds 70 per cent of the shares, and Juan holds 30 per cent of the shares, in their personal names. They are both in their mid-forties and work full time in the business, which they established five years ago.

After five successful years growing the business, Juan is diagnosed with cancer and dies six months later. In his will, Juan leaves all of his property (including his shares in SJ Construction) to his wife Rita. Rita is a nurse by training, and has been a stay-at-home mum for the last nine years. She had always been supportive of Juan's career, but knows little about the business or the construction world.

This situation creates a problem for both Sarah and Rita.

From Sarah's perspective, she now co-owns a business with someone whom she does not know particularly well, and who does not have the skills or contacts to take over Juan's executive role.

From Rita's perspective, she now owns an illiquid share in a closely held private company. She does not understand the business, and is unable to devote any meaningful time or attention to it.

Sarah would like to buy Rita out, but does not have the available capital and the business does not have sufficient assets to borrow against. Sarah and Rita also have a different opinion as to how much Rita's 30 per cent shareholding is worth. Juan had always told Rita that the business was extremely profitable, and its prospects were good. However, because Juan

was a very skilled marketer, Sarah is concerned that the business will suffer following his death, and has a more conservative opinion as to what it is worth. Rita, in turn, is sceptical that Sarah is just looking to buy out her 30 per cent share for the lowest price possible.

Six months after Juan's death, the relationship between Sarah and Rita becomes strained. They are both still suffering from the grief and shock of losing Juan. Sarah has a big workload just trying to keep everything going without Juan's contribution. Rita is worried and suspicious, as she doesn't know or understand what Sarah is doing in the business. Sarah and Rita soon fall out.

Rita seeks legal advice. As a result of that advice, she insists on calling regular shareholders meetings to understand the business better and ensure that Sarah remains accountable. Rita attends those meetings with her lawyer, which Sarah finds extremely antagonistic. At the shareholders meetings, Rita's lawyer always asks difficult questions about the business, and this soaks up even more of Sarah's time in preparing for the meetings.

Because Juan is no longer around and Sarah is so distracted, the revenue and profitability of SJ Construction decline significantly over the year following Juan's death. Rita tries to introduce a competitor who has offered to buy both shareholders out. Sarah refuses.

The situation is resolved after Rita's lawyer applies to the court to wind up SJ Construction and liquidate its assets – a final and drastic way of resolving their differences. Deeply concerned by this aggressive approach, Sarah borrows against her home to make an increased offer for Rita's 30 per cent share. The offer is for substantially more than what Sarah believes the shareholding is worth, but is less than what Rita had originally requested. Rita begrudgingly accepts. By this time, both Sarah and Rita have also incurred significant legal costs.

How could Sarah and Juan have better managed their affairs to avoid such an unsatisfactory outcome?

The key mistake that Juan and Sarah made is that they did not put in place a shareholders agreement to govern unplanned succession. That agreement could have provided that the death of one shareholder would trigger the forced sale of their shares to the other shareholder. A clause of that nature would have given Sarah the ability to control 100 per cent of the business, and allowed Rita to 'cash in' the value of Juan's shareholding following Juan's death.

If Sarah and Juan had put in place a shareholders agreement containing a clause of this nature, they would have needed to consider the following issues:

1. What would be the purchase price for Juan's shares upon death? In particular, would the shares be independently valued as at the date of death? If so, should the valuer apply a pre-determined valuation formula – for example, 3.5 times the last financial year's profits?

2. Should a discount be applied to the valuation to reflect that Juan holds an illiquid minority interest in a private company? If so, how big a discount?

3. When should the purchase price for the shares be paid – for example, will it all be paid up front, or over a period of time?

Sarah and Juan should have also considered obtaining 'ownership protection' insurance, to fund the payment for each other's shares in SJ Construction upon their death or total and permanent disablement. This insurance can be extremely useful. It means that, amongst all of the other painful issues, at least the surviving shareholder does not have to find the money to buy out the other shareholder at a time which is very difficult for all concerned. Sometimes, the insurance can also extend to so-called 'trauma events' such as suffering a stroke or heart attack.

Once ownership protection insurance has been put in place, you should review the level of cover each year. As the business grows and becomes more valuable, the amount of your insurance cover will need to increase or there will be a shortfall upon death.

Another clause that might have been useful in the shareholders agreement would have been a requirement for the company to obtain 'key person' insurance over the lives of Sarah and Juan. Unlike ownership protection insurance, where the respective shareholders are the beneficiaries, the beneficiary under a 'key person' policy is the company itself. In this way, SJ Constructions would have received some additional cash to compensate it for the loss of Juan's efforts as a marketer in the time between his death and recruiting another person to his executive position.

The second case study examines how the poor performance of one business owner can create succession issues:

Elite Engineering

Damian, Gareth, Tom and Sinead are shareholders in a consulting engineering company called Elite Engineering.

Damian set up Elite Engineering 20 years ago, and in recent years sold some of his shares to senior employees Gareth, Tom and Sinead. The shareholdings are now as follows – Damian 35 per cent, Gareth 35 per cent, Tom 20 per cent and Sinead 10 per cent. There is no shareholders agreement in relation to Elite Engineering, and none of the four shareholders have employment contracts.

Gareth is the managing director of Elite Engineering, and each of Damian, Tom and Sinead work as consultants/project managers.

Damian's work performance has significantly deteriorated in recent times. A highly talented engineer, he seems to have lost interest in the business since his marriage ended two years ago. He is also independently wealthy and does not need to work full time for a living. Damian spends a lot of his time on business trips (ostensibly marketing to potential new clients, but with patchy results), hosting long lunches and trading options online.

The other shareholders have endeavoured to discuss their concerns with Damian, but to no avail. Elite Engineering's profitability is declining, and they feel that they are unable to 'carry' Damian any more, particularly given his significant salary and profit share.

One day, Gareth approaches Damian once more to discuss his performance and motivation at work. Damian responds by saying he knows that Gareth, Tom and Sinead have been 'out to get him' for some time; they are greedy and have forgotten that it was Damian who gave them the opportunity to become shareholders in the first place. Gareth tries to explain his concerns about Damian's performance, but Damian reacts angrily and storms out.

A week passes, and Damian does not return to work. Damian then tenders his resignation as an employee and managing director of Elite Engineering. He gives one month's notice, and during that period does not come into the office.

Following the termination of his employment, Damian promptly sets up a competing business and starts approaching the client base of Elite Engineering. He also approaches certain key staff members of Elite Engineering, offering them more money to join his new business. Damian, of course, remains a 35 per cent shareholder in Elite Engineering. The other shareholders issue legal proceedings against Damian, seeking to restrain him from further damaging their business.

While Damian's behaviour and work performance have been extremely poor, it is unfortunately Gareth, Tom and Sinead who have the weaker position in the ensuing litigation. This is because:

- They have no shareholders agreement which gives them the right to purchase Damian's shares.

- Damian has no employment contract and is not bound by any restraint-of-trade obligations preventing him from establishing a competing business or soliciting clients following the termination of his employment. Damian was also careful not to solicit the clients, or take steps to establish his competing business, while he remained an employee of Elite Engineering.

- Damian has the rights to continue to receive dividends, attend and vote at shareholders meetings, receive financial information about Elite Engineering, and not be oppressed in his capacity as a minority shareholder. He starts to assert these rights in an aggressive manner, aiming to cause as much hassle and discomfort for the other shareholders as possible.

Damian also brings a counterclaim against Elite Engineering, alleging that he was frozen out by his co-shareholders and 'constructively dismissed' from his employment.

In order to acquire Damian's shares and bring an end to the acrimonious dispute, Gareth, Tom and Sinead end up paying him a very large sum of money. They then pay him an additional sum in return for Damian agreeing to sign a limited restraint-of-trade clause. This clause allows Damian to continue with his separate business, but prevents him from soliciting certain clients and employees of Elite Engineering for a period of 6 months.

In a similar way to the previous case study, many of the troubles experienced by Gareth, Tom and Sinead could have been avoided with a robust shareholders agreement and employment contract. The time for them to negotiate these agreements would have been when they were negotiating to buy their shares from Damian (and therefore had maximum leverage).

Gareth, Tom and Sinead learned their lesson, and following the settlement with Damian promptly put in place a shareholders agreement. It is ironic that the cost of that shareholders agreement was significantly less than the legal fees that they spent pursuing Damian through the courts.

KEY LEARNINGS FROM THIS CHAPTER:

- If you co-own a business with one or more other people, a shareholders agreement is crucial to protect you.

- Your shareholders agreement should contain clear exit mechanisms that govern both planned and unplanned succession.

- Always consider whether ownership protection insurance and/or key person insurance can assist. Your financial planner can advise you about this.

Chapter 10

Your professional team and the value of good advice

In this chapter you will learn

how to get the most out of your professional advisers

and

where many business owners get it wrong

Why good advice is important

Given that I earn a living from advising business owners on exit strategies, it is perhaps unsurprising that this book extols the virtues of appointing good people to assist you!

That said, whilst I acknowledge my own vested interest, please be aware that selecting good advisers and managing them properly is critical to the success of your business succession strategy. These strategies are often complex and difficult to execute. You normally only have one chance to get it right, and the implications of getting it wrong can be huge.

I have seen many business owners progress an exit strategy without proper professional advice. This jeopardises their succession plan and can mean that they do not exit for full value.

For this reason, when writing this book I felt strongly that it was important to provide you with some guidance on this subject.

Where business owners get it wrong

From a professional advice perspective, the most common mistakes are:

- not getting any tax advice
- tax advice being sought too late in the process
- advisers not communicating

No tax advice

If you don't get good tax advice on your exit strategy, it can cost you an awful lot of money. This is unfortunately an extremely common mistake for private or family business owners.

It always makes me shudder when I hear about yet another business owner who was completely ignorant of the tax treatment of their sale and ended up lining the tax man's pockets.

There are many legitimate ways in which tax can be minimised on the sale of your business. Because the law is so dynamic and complex in this area, a detailed analysis is outside the scope of this book.

Good tax advisers are expensive due to their high levels of knowledge and their ability to apply complex taxation laws to commercial transactions. Their advice can generate significant tax savings. Please take heed and put your hand in your pocket for quality tax advice. *You have been warned!*

Tax advice provided too late in the process

Continuing on the same theme, another common error is to seek tax advice too late in a sale process.

For example, you may structure the divestment of your business as an asset sale, and create an offer letter and other documents to reflect this. However, following the initial negotiations with the buyer, you obtain some advice and become aware that you would achieve a much better tax result by selling the entire issued share capital of your company. The offer letter and sale documents are therefore changed, a share sale transaction is concluded and you complete and lodge your tax return accordingly.

The risk in this is the effect of the anti-avoidance provisions of the tax legislation. If you are ever audited by the tax authorities, they may question why your transaction started its life as an asset sale, but then mysteriously changed to a share sale at a late stage. If the reason for this was to avoid tax (with no genuine non-tax reason for the change in the sale structure) then depending on the circumstances those authorities could pursue you for the additional tax together with penalties and interest.

If you had obtained good advice earlier, the transaction could perhaps have been structured differently from the outset.

Advisers not communicating

In order to get the best results from your team of professional advisers, it is important to facilitate and encourage them to work together.

If you are overly concerned about minimising professional costs, you may keep your advisers operating in 'silos', not communicating with each other and each working on a precisely defined individual task. This is a mistake.

Instead, in my experience the most powerful 'value add' is derived when you get your lawyer, accountant, tax adviser and other relevant adviser(s) in the room together with yourself, and spend some time workshopping the relevant issues.

You will find this to be an interesting process as the advisers will never agree on everything and, indeed, may have wildly differing views on certain subjects! However, from these different perspectives come the best ideas and creative solutions. It is extremely powerful to have your entire advisory team challenge each other's thinking in this manner.

It is important during a session like this for your advisers to leave their egos at the door. Any adviser who does not respect the views of another may not be a good fit for your team.

Succession story – Joanne

Ten years ago, Joanne set up a suburban pub/restaurant. Joanne put up half the capital, and the executive chef put up the other half. They co-owned the business on a 50/50 basis.

The business was successful. Joanne repeated this approach many times over, each time co-investing with a different executive chef who would run the pub/restaurant in question. There are now nine pub/restaurants in the group.

Joanne's game plan from the outset was to sell all of the businesses to a large public company. She perceived that this exit strategy might realise significantly more value than selling off each pub/restaurant individually.

When establishing the pub/restaurants with each of her co-owners, Joanne was careful to put in place a shareholders agreement which gives her the right to procure an exit of the entire group, either by trade sale or IPO, subject to certain conditions being fulfilled. This right is conditional upon the sale of each pub/restaurant being for a certain minimum earnings multiple.

Without such a document, it would be near impossible to sell the group as a whole, as this would require the consent of each of the individual co-owners.

The shareholders agreement also provides Joanne with a first right of refusal should any of her co-owners wish to sell their share in a business.

Joanne has successfully kept her future options open, and is now able to represent the group with confidence when she approaches (or is approached by) potential buyers.

Selecting a professional advisory team

The core professional advisory team for your exit strategy will normally be as follows:

1. *Lead or strategic adviser.* This person reviews your business and advises you on the various succession options, timing and strategy. They may then be retained to go to the market and find a buyer, and generally take a lead role in the negotiations. For larger transactions, the lead or strategic adviser is generally a corporate finance accountant or investment banker. For smaller transactions, another adviser may take the lead role.

2. ***Accountant.*** The accountant assists with business valuation, and prepares or collates the historical financial information and any necessary financial projections. They may also review the financial aspects of the sale documentation, including any formulae or other mechanisms for determining or adjusting the sale price.

3. ***Lawyer.*** The lawyer assists in minimising risk in connection with your exit strategy. They prepare and advise upon the necessary legal documents, processes and legal liabilities. They may also take responsibility for process management and 'stage managing' completion. A lawyer can also assist you with asset protection strategies.

4. ***Tax adviser.*** This person is generally a specialist lawyer or accountant. They advise on the structuring and tax consequences of the transaction.

5. ***Financial planner.*** The financial planner assists you to invest the proceeds of your exit strategy to achieve your financial goals and lifestyle objectives. They also help you to make sensible investment decisions along the way, to ensure that your personal wealth is not all tied up in your business. Another important role is to help reduce the financial pain of an unplanned exit through death or total and permanent disablement, by advising on appropriate insurance arrangements.

In my view, when selecting a professional adviser, websites and other marketing materials are generally of little use. Business succession has become something of a 'buzzword', and professional services firms of all shapes and sizes will make bold claims as to their experience and expertise in this area.

The best endorsement comes from others who have used the services of an adviser for their own exit strategy. When interviewing professional advisers, you should therefore ask for the contact details of client referees for whom they have provided similar services in the past. If those advisers are reluctant to do this, or cannot give concrete examples of other similar matters that they have worked on, this should start the 'warning bells' ringing.

The question of fees can also be telling. In this area, the maxim that 'you get what you pay for' holds true. You should therefore be wary if an adviser provides a quotation that is significantly lower than the market rate. This generally indicates that they do not consider their own advice to be particularly valuable, or that they do not have a good grasp of the amount of work that is required.

Managing your professional advisory team

A business sale or other exit is often one of the most significant events in your life. It is likely to involve levels of professional advice, assistance and planning that you have never before experienced. And, amongst all of this activity, you still need to keep the business running!

While the professional advisers will look after various key aspects of the project, it is important that you are mentally engaged with the process and manage the advisers effectively. Some ways in which this should be done are as follows:

- Ensure that you have clear, written arrangements in place which describe the scope of each adviser's work and the fee (or estimated fee) that will be paid for that work. Ask that they update you promptly if they anticipate that their fees may exceed the estimated range.

- Do not try to short-change your advisers by asking them to enter into aggressively low fee arrangements, pushing them to provide additional services for free or paying them outside their stated payment terms. An adviser who is treated in this manner is unlikely to give 100 per cent to the assignment, and may end up feeling resentful of the business owner and the job in hand. This may also lead the adviser to inappropriately delegate the matter to junior staff members, or do the minimum work possible without any 'value add'.

- Ensure that there are no gaps or duplication between the services provided by the various advisers. For example, the law firm and the accountancy firm may each erroneously assume that the other one is providing you with tax advice. Or, they may both involve their respective tax teams, which results in double the fees. This largely comes down to good communication between yourself and the advisory team.

- Remember that, at the end of the day, you are the client. If you are not comfortable with a course of action, are being kept in the dark, or feel that you are being inappropriately 'pushed' to sell (or not to sell), then say so. If your advisers do not respond positively or change their behaviour, consider changing them.

It is also interesting to bear in mind the basis upon which your professional advisers are remunerated. I was once at a negotiation meeting, representing the seller of a large financial services business. The time had come to plan the sequence of action points that were required in order to finalise the sale agreement and complete the transaction. The investment bankers on both sides were pushing for an aggressive timetable that would see the deal completed within the week. However, the lawyers on both sides argued that this was a complex matter and that more time was required to cover off various issues properly. The CEO of the buyer company said, with a smile, *'What a surprise. The advisers who are paid a success fee want the deal to happen quickly, but the advisers who are paid on hourly rates want to string it out!'*

This was, of course, a light-hearted comment made at the end of a long day. Most advisers are extremely professional, and would not allow such factors to affect their judgement or advice. However, this story does serve as a reminder to be aware of the basis upon which you remunerate your advisers, and the behaviours that this may drive.

KEY LEARNINGS FROM THIS CHAPTER:

- Invest in good tax advice early in your business succession process.

- Encourage your professional advisers to work inclusively together. A good way to do this is to get all of them in the same room to workshop key issues.

- Always be proactive in managing your advisory team. In particular, ensure that there are no gaps or duplication in their services.

- Remember that you are the boss. If your advisers do not heed your instructions or 'pull their head in' when necessary, let them know and take steps to address this.

Chapter 11

Negotiating

In this chapter you will learn

key negotiation skills and techniques to maximise value on the sale of your business

Negotiation techniques

In my career I have seen many business owners carefully plan for the sale of their business, but then *fall at the final hurdle through failing to negotiate a good deal with the buyer.*

As a business owner, you may not be a skilful negotiator. Or, even if you are, the personal or sensitive nature of some of these discussions may make you emotional and therefore dangerous at the negotiating table.

Set out below are some basic techniques that should assist you in getting the best deal when it comes to negotiating the price and terms of your sale transaction.

Price negotiations

A common mistake is to *propose a price* to potential buyers rather than to *invite offers.*

Take this example. Fred is looking to sell his business to Brigitte. In anticipation of the sale process, Fred has his business independently valued in the sum of $2 million. Brigitte does her due diligence, and is keen to progress with the negotiations. Brigitte asks Fred what his asking price is. Fred says $2.2 million (a comfortable excess above the independent valuation).

What Fred has just done by proposing a price to Brigitte, even though it is at the high end, is to effectively put a cap on the maximum amount that she will ever pay. Who knows, there may be some particular synergy or other reason why the business is actually worth $3 million to Brigitte!

The better approach would have been for Fred to simply counter Brigitte's request with an invitation for her to make an offer. In that way, he will understand the low-end parameter from her perspective, and should then be able to negotiate the price up without being the one to first 'show his hand'.

Similarly, it is important for Fred to know (but of course never reveal) his reserve or 'walk away' price.

Standing your ground

You may be surprised by the formal and sometimes aggressive nature of business sale negotiations, particularly when lawyers are involved. Some lawyers are badly behaved and downright rude; others just get carried away with the 'cut and thrust' of the debate. Either way, their antics may cause you concern. *It is fine to tell your lawyer to hold back or (dare I say it!) shut up on occasions.*

Because you are out of your comfort zone in this environment, you may be tempted to make concessions simply to bring an end to the 'unpleasantness' of the discussions. This is a mistake. Sometimes, standing your ground is really important. The trick is to do this, wherever possible, in a way which gives the prospective buyer some options and 'get outs'. In this way, they are not made to feel they are being backed into a corner.

Point scoring

Some people see the negotiation process as one of 'point scoring'. In other words, they count the number of points that they have 'won' in the negotiation as against the number that they have 'lost'. I have sometimes heard lawyers and other professional negotiators boast to their clients and colleagues that 'We won nine out of the ten outstanding points'.

The better approach is usually to stand firm on the issues that are important to you, but to compromise on the issues that are less important. It makes little sense to 'win' nine points that are of little importance, but then to 'lose' the only point that is of real commercial significance.

Speak less, listen more

Some of the best negotiators that I have seen are very good at knowing when to say nothing.

Rather than having a big personality and 'grandstanding' in the negotiation, these clever operators will spend the majority of the meeting humbly sitting back, listening, and absorbing the arguments made by others. Then they will make one incredibly perceptive point that nails the issue.

One benefit of this approach is that when you say nothing, it is impossible to make a concession! On the other hand, those who say a lot will often find themselves making concessions or letting slip a fact or opinion which results in them giving away some negotiating leverage.

Make concessions wisely

Skilful negotiators seek to use concessions to extract some benefit for themselves, rather than simply giving them away.

For example, if you intend to concede on three points but wish to stay firm on the fourth, one approach might be to offer the three concessions as a 'package' in exchange for the fourth point.

That said, a skilful person on the other side might say that they are not interested in horse-trading, and that instead each point must be considered, discussed and agreed on its merits.

Use a professional

There is a reason why good investment bankers and corporate advisors are able to charge decent success fees – they are often able to secure a significantly better deal than if you were to fly solo.

This is partly due to their network of contacts and ability to find a buyer, but it is also due to their refined negotiation skills. After all, these advisers earn a living from negotiating sale transactions, whereas you may only do so once in your lifetime.

It can also sometimes be useful for you to 'hide behind' an adviser, who can say all of the difficult things that you may be reluctant to put forward. When I was a trainee lawyer, a senior colleague told me never to be afraid of being the youngest person in the negotiation meeting. This is because clients sometimes like to have a young, aggressive adviser who will 'put themselves out there' and say all of the nasty things that the client does not want to mention!

KEY LEARNINGS FROM THIS CHAPTER:

- Invite offers rather than propose a sale price.
- Stand your ground where necessary, but do so in a way which will allow the buyer to save face or agree a compromise position.
- Do not engage in point scoring; stick to the issues that are important to you and compromise on the others.
- Avoid saying too much – you will talk yourself into making concessions.
- Unless you are a highly skilled negotiator, consider using a corporate adviser or other professional to undertake the lead negotiations on your behalf.

Chapter 12

Progressing your exit strategy

In this chapter you will learn

why business owners fail to plan for ownership succession

and

practical hints and tips to start your succession planning journey

Failure to plan

Here's the paradox. *Whilst most business owners acknowledge the need for good succession planning, in practice they are **shockingly bad** at actually doing it.*

Take a look at yourself. On one level you might be attracted by some of the strategies in this book. But how many of them will you actually follow through with? Perhaps you will just throw yourself back into your everyday workload, resolving to think about them another day. Like a hamster on the wheel, your life will once again become consumed by the so-called important everyday business issues, with little time given to the really big stuff – the plans that could revolutionise your future.

This chapter looks at the reasons why so many business owners do not have a succession plan, and why most of those who have one fail to carry it out.

And, whilst there are no easy answers, I will provide you with some practical hints and tips on how to devote time to progressing your business succession strategy.

The reasons

The reasons that I hear from those who fail to plan for succession are many and varied. Here are some of them:

- *'There is no need for me to groom my business for sale. I will simply give the* business to my son/daughter/children/son-in-law [delete as applicable] *when the time is right.'*

- *'Why do I need to think about business succession? I am only in my [thirties/forties/fifties/sixties]'* [delete as applicable]

- *'But I do have a plan. My employees will buy me out in five years. Those guys can't wait to push me off the perch and get their hands on my equity. Then they will realise what running a business is all about!'*

- *'Hmm, business succession, that's really important. We talk about this issue all the time at my CEO group. That said, I am too busy looking after my customers right now. Let's discuss next [month/year/decade].'* [delete as applicable]

- *'I have big private equity funds calling me all the time looking to buy this business. I refuse to return their calls. It won't be any trouble for me to sell when the time comes.'*

- *'I have no assets other than my business. I will need to keep working for many more years to grow this business – it is my retirement fund.'*

- *'Without me in the business, it's worth nothing anyway. So why bother with succession planning?'*

If we were able to scratch beneath the surface and hear the true reasons behind these flawed statements, they might actually be as follows:

- *'I have spent the last 30 years successfully building this business. I derive my self-identity and sense of worth from being a business owner. Selling the business would create a huge void in my life.'*

- *'I am scared of stopping work. My wife and I would drive each other crazy, and there is only so much golf you can play.'*

- *'No-one else can run this business like I do. I have poured my heart and soul into making it a success. And besides, my customers have become personal friends.'*

The failure to address these issues is emotionally, and not logically, driven. It involves confronting not only your retirement, but also your mortality and the essence of your being. It is no wonder that many business owners 'make the right noises' about transitioning their business or taking the next step, but then when the crunch comes they change their mind or procrastinate.

It is similar to the reason why people delay making a will. Everyone knows that they should do it, but it is difficult and painful to confront what the future may hold. Combine this with the fact that there is always something more immediate and pressing to do, and the path of least resistance is to simply ignore it and plough on regardless.

In his fantastic book 'Strategy and the Fat Smoker'[1], David Maister draws an analogy between strategic planning and making new year's resolutions. The issue lies not in making the resolution, but in keeping it. In both our personal lives and in business, we all know what is best for us – giving up smoking, drinking less, exercising more, planning for succession, the list goes on. Maister explains that the problem with human beings is that we are not good at delaying gratification – we don't want to put in the hard work now for a benefit that will only be received years down the track.

Getting focussed

So, how do you get focussed on business succession? Here are a few thoughts.

Reflect on and write down your life goals

Before you can formulate a business succession plan, you should spend some time reflecting on your life goals (in the broadest sense, not just financial). These life goals will be different for every business owner. They might include a broad range of things such as travel plans, establishing or promoting a charity or other foundation, buying and developing real property, spending time with grandchildren, setting up a new business venture, seeking a portfolio of non-executive company directorships or ensuring that family members are looked after financially.

Only once you know what you are aiming for can you start planning for how to achieve it! By writing down your life goals, this will provide valuable thoughts which will dovetail into your business ownership strategy. It will also start you thinking about how much money you will need to fund those goals.

*While this may sound overly deep or 'spiritual', your business succession planning journey therefore needs to start with the fundamental question of **what do I want to achieve with my life?***

In a holistic manner, you can then build the achievement of your business succession strategy into the broader strategy for your life and business.

Tell someone

Once you have thought about your plans and goals, it is time to tell someone. Committing to a course of action is much easier when you have someone to keep you accountable.

I know one senior business owner who has written the *precise date of his retirement* in big black pen on his office whiteboard for all to see. It fires him up to count down the days and years and plan for his succession, and his whiteboard serves as a constant reminder to staff of the challenges and opportunities that lie ahead. Having published his plans to the world, it will be difficult for him to change his mind when the time comes!

Or, one of my business partners has thrown down the gauntlet to his senior staff, telling them *'if you don't replace me in three years, I will replace you'*.

Seek the right assistance

If the reason for failing to confront business ownership succession is primarily emotional, then one way to get focussed is to engage a professional who understands and can assist with these emotional issues.

Some useful assistance at the early stages of the succession planning process may come from a professional such as a financial planner, a trusted business coach or a psychologist. These professionals often have good 'soft' skills such as the ability to listen and empathise, and do not deal exclusively in the world of hard facts and figures. Financial planners and business coaches in particular spend their professional lives setting goals and looking at future plans and aspirations for their clients.

While it is also crucial to discuss your business succession plans with family members, you should recognise that they may sometimes not be best placed to help you in the early stages.

Family members may have personal or vested interests in the outcome of your decision (for example, your son or daughter may wish to own or manage the business one day, or conversely they may be hoping that you sell the business quickly to diversify the family's wealth). Or, they may simply be too emotionally close to provide the necessary objectivity.

Plan for your life post-business succession

Most of the planning and professional advice that is given in connection with business succession relates to the 'pointy end' – the actual sale process.

Business succession advice is therefore transactionally driven. It is rarely the case that any attention is given to the important question of 'what next' for the business owner.

This is, in my view, a flaw in most business succession planning processes. Without a clear vision or path for the post-succession world, you may be less engaged with the process or your judgement may become clouded by non-business issues.

The question of 'what next' could include any number of roles either inside or outside the business. You should take time to plan for the next stage of your life and career before embarking on a business succession process.

If you are not excited about the next stage, how can you ever expect to stop procrastinating and execute a successful business succession plan?

KEY LEARNINGS FROM THIS CHAPTER:

- Acknowledge the true reason(s) behind your failure to implement a business succession plan, and work with a business coach, financial planner, psychologist, or other suitably qualified professional to address this.

- Write down your goals and actively plan for your life following exit.

- If you are not excited about the next phase, you will never progress your exit strategy.

---

1   David Maister 2008 'Strategy and the Fat Smoker: doing what's obvious but not easy' – Spangle Press.

Chapter 13

Bringing it all together: the five steps to sell for a 'super profit'

This chapter brings together the key learnings of this book

The five steps

I hope that this book has inspired you to look at your business in a different way, and motivated you to set the foundations for your exit strategy.

This final chapter draws together the ideas from earlier chapters, and distils them into the five steps to sell for a super profit. I call them 'the five Ps'.

The five steps are as follows:

1. *Preparation* – prepare your business for sale by completing the basics in Chapter 3.
2. *Premium value drivers* – create a business which has one or more of the premium value drivers referred to in Chapter 4.
3. *Purchaser* – identify possible buyers early, and develop relationships with them.
4. *Projections* – prepare credible financial projections to support the future growth expectations of your business, and persuade the buyer to pay for that future growth based on those projections.
5. *Pre-emption* – ensure you that you pre-empt and take steps to mitigate any health, financial or other non-business issues which may force you to sell at the wrong time.

In practice, your plan should look something like this:

Step 1: Preparation

In the three years or so before you intend to exit, ensure that your business can demonstrate the basic requirements such as quality financial records and reporting, an appropriate corporate structure, and clear legal rights to important assets.

Do not shy away from the fact that this will involve putting your hand in your pocket to work closely with your professional advisers during this period. You should pay for good advice now, ensure that you follow that advice, and take solace in the fact that this is an investment which will pay dividends when it comes time to sell.

Work with your accountant to ensure that high quality monthly, quarterly and annual financials are in place.

Do what you can to grow the earnings of the business in the years before sale, in a supportable and sustainable manner. Time it right so that your business is profitable and ha160

s a great growth story at the time you exit.

Step 2: Premium value drivers

Ensure that your business develops one or more of the 'big four' premium value drivers, which you may recall are:

- lack of principal dependency (and with key personnel 'locked in')
- sustainable competitive advantage
- strong governance systems
- being a strategic acquisition target for your competitors

Step 3: Purchaser(s)

Throughout the early preparation stages, seek out and develop relationships with potential buyers for your business.

Step 4: Projections

Prepare detailed and supportable financial projections to provide to the buyer. Ensure that these projections are credible by:

- implementing a detailed annual budgeting process in the years before sale
- where possible, locking in revenues and expenses through robust long term contracts
- where possible, creating a business based on solid recurring revenue streams.

Step 5: Pre-emption

Do not devote your life to your business to the extent that your health suffers and forces you to sell. Block time out in your diary to exercise and get up early in the morning to do this if necessary. Also ensure that you take regular medical check ups.

If your business has co-owners, put in place a shareholders agreement to govern both planned and unplanned succession.

Consider mitigating the business risks of ill health through ownership protection

FIVE ACTION POINTS TO GET YOU STARTED

1. Complete the Exit Strategy Checklist at the back of this book.

2. Arrange a meeting with your family or business partners, show them the completed Exit Strategy Checklist and discuss your future aspirations.

3. Review your net asset position generally. Think about whether you need to grow and diversify your asset base to achieve your financial goals.

4. Ask your professional advisers for their thoughts about the future of your business and exit strategy.

5. Reflect upon, and write down, your life goals.

Interviews

Tom McKaskill
and Katalin Johnson

Mark Emerson

Philippa Taylor

Alan Rodway

Tom McKaskill and Katalin Johnson

Dr Tom McKaskill is a global serial entrepreneur, consultant, educator and author. He has successfully sold several businesses, and is acknowledged as the world's leading authority on exit strategies for high growth enterprises.

Katalin Johnson is Tom's life partner and works closely with him on his projects. She has contributed to, and edited, many of Tom's publications.

How should sellers prepare their business for sale?

Tom: Sellers always need to come back to the question of 'why is the buyer going to make a lot of money out of my business?'

When you sell a business, the more you can understand about the buyer, the better you are able to position yourself for a sale. This is what most sellers don't do – *they don't get inside the buyer's head.*

Once you have figured out who the buyer will be and how they are going to make money out of your business, then you can work out what you need to do to make your business attractive to that buyer.

Katalin: The lead-in time to exit is really important. If sellers have not been through this process and want to sell immediately, that's hard.

Tom: It is certainly a long preparation period. If you only have three months to do this, you're dead. But, if you have two years to prepare, it makes a huge difference.

So, you need to turn your business into a strategic acquisition target for buyers?

Tom: Yes. Most sellers are working on a 1970s and 1980s growth model. This means that they are focussed on multiples of EBIT and the like.

Katalin: That is the tradition – it is what we all learned. But it is important to realise that some businesses can 'break the mould'. What is really exciting about Tom's work is that it involves developing a framework or process to help more businesses fall into this exceptional category.

Tom: Historical profit growth is certainly likely to be an indicator of what the business will do in future if it continues to have the same product/market position and be managed the same way. But, sellers should take a different view. They should find a buyer who can do a lot of things with the business that the seller is unable to – for example, provide distribution channels that the seller is unable to get into.

Katalin: For this reason, when talking to sellers we tend not to talk about multiples of EBIT. This just clouds people's ability to make the paradigm shift. What we want them to think about is how they can change the future.

What are the special factors that give a business owner the best chance to sell for a super-profit?

Tom: The main factors are a high compelling need for the products or services of the business, a high sustainable competitive advantage, clearly identified customers, good distribution channels, and a product or service that is scalable or easily replicated.

Katalin: Of these, scalability is important. Scalability means very high growth rates for the buyer after they have bought the business.

Tom: As an example, we have been recently looking at a technology business.

That business has a lot going for it – its products are the 'best of breed', and there is interest in those products from large companies all over the world. But, the products are very complex and you need to train the sales staff to a high level before they can sell them effectively. And, the customers only re-tender for this type of product infrequently, so it has a 12-month sales cycle. So, if you are the buyer of this business, you need to fund the sales cycle and that's a lot of funding.

So, whilst this business is good, *it has a scalability problem.*

It is easy to be caught up in the sustainable competitive advantage of a business, but not look at the speed of scalability.

How else can sellers maximise the value of their business?

Tom: Well, they can sell the same business twice.

Katalin: Or, three or four times.

152

Excuse me, but how does that work.......?!

Katalin: Well, your business may have different components that you can spin off to different buyers who are best placed to exploit those particular components.

Or, you could licence the same product many times over, in different geographic regions.

Tom: Or, you can develop a product with many different applications that can be sold into different markets that do not overlap. For example, the same core technology could have applications in both agriculture and medicine.

So, it is quite true – in this way you can actually sell the same company more than once. Buyers only pay for what they can effectively exploit. So if you have a capability in two different markets, it is best to find two buyers – one for each separate market.

Mark Emerson

Mark is the Managing Director of Sustained Ability, a management consulting firm that works with business leaders to build sustained business improvement and profitability.

Before establishing Sustained Ability, Mark founded, grew and successfully divested his interest in a well-known recruitment business.

What advice would you give business owners who are looking to transition their business to the management team?

For business owners, the 'letting go' piece is often a really big issue.

If you initiate a transition that involves selling part of your business to the management team, you are getting paid to let go. *So, let go!* There is a commercial reality associated with it.

And before embarking on the transition, there needs to be a thorough process of interrogation and agreement as to what 'letting go' really means to all parties. If possible, the agreement regarding ongoing roles in the business is ideally documented in the shareholders agreement.

What does that process entail?

Establishing the roles and responsibilities of all involved in the buy-out is really important.

The business owner might say *'I am going to sell 50% to you, and I will become the Chairman and step away from the coal face'.* But then after the sale the owner still does exactly what they have always done, run the business.

The solution is for all parties to participate in a formal process of re-scoping the roles. This often gets missed. Everyone talks about the sale price, multiples, and the like, but this re-scoping process is a priority. The tighter one can document the respective roles and responsibilities, the more effectively all parties will contribute post the equity transition. It will also help in managing everyone's expectations.

The other big thing is all about how decisions get made during the period of co-ownership. The risk is any party adopting the often emotional position of *'I will still do what I always used to do'.* In these situations, problems emerge for all parties, particularly when the original owner doesn't change their behaviour to accommodate the aspirations of the new equity participants.

Again, it's an ideal outcome when all parties think about the ongoing framework for decision making, agree how it will work and document it in the shareholders agreement.

Adopting these initiatives will enable everyone to identify and remedy common catalysts for potential disputes before they get too nasty. A shareholders agreement is not an exact science, but the more detail that is captured within it the better.

Does anything else often get missed?

Taking out insurance to fund the buyout of beneficiaries should a partner die during the transition often gets missed. People just don't think about it. Whenever an additional shareholder is taken on, all parties need to be able to buy out the deceased shareholder's beneficiaries. Otherwise the business may risk a forced sale to realise assets to pay them out. The shareholders agreement should also transparently define the action taken should a shareholder die during transition.

Another smart move is to source independent input from a trusted adviser. There are two people that will ideally be really close to you through transition. One is a good accountant. The other is a trusted adviser who can act as an independent director or sounding board during the period of transition for all parties to access in dispute resolution.

How should you select a candidate for a staged succession?

Particularly in services industries, people may offer equity to the best salesperson or longest serving employees because of the contribution they are making to the business. However being around the longest or being best in one discipline doesn't qualify that person to be a good future CEO. Think hard about whether that person can step up and become the business leader that the company needs them to be.

Also, when considering candidates for equity, for some it is just about the numbers. But there may be no cultural fit, and that can lead to disaster. The cultural piece is every bit as critical as the financial and business fit and the investment in evaluating it should not be overlooked.

Any final thoughts for business owners on succession strategies?

Succession should never be the catalyst for strategy. Succession is an outcome of strategy.

This means that anyone who is smart about the way they operate their business and protect their investment will have a succession plan as *an integral part of their broader business strategy*. If there's no strategy and no succession plan, then good luck!

Philippa Taylor

Philippa is the Chief Executive Officer of Family Business Australia ('FBA'), the peak body for family and private business in Australia.

How effectively do family businesses prepare for succession?

Well, most of them are simply not prepared at all.

Approximately 74% of the businesses in Australia are family-owned, but only 27% have a written succession plan.

Why are they so under-prepared?

Well, we know that these people aren't stupid. If they were, they wouldn't be successful business people. In FBA's experience, the main reasons are as follows.

First, the next generation has not done a good job of breaching the generation gap and proving that they are ready, willing and able to take on the business. It is also difficult for them to raise issues like *'Dad, do you have a will?',* especially where significant sums of money are involved. So, from the next generation's perspective, they may be ready to take over the business, but have never communicated this effectively to their parents.

Secondly, it has a lot to do with the founder's sense of identity and sense of purpose. The chances are that Dad has been working in the business eleven hours a day, six and a half days a week. He hasn't learned to fish or play golf, he hasn't had the time. He doesn't know what to do in his retirement, so why would he retire? His position is different to those executives in the corporate world who have had more of a life outside their work.

Another reason many business owners hang on past their `sell by date' is that they have failed to prepare financially for their retirement, and lack confidence in leaving their security in the hands of the next generation. Many have ploughed earnings back into the business, and have neglected their superannuation. Timely and good financial advice can be a key to freeing up the business owner to let the next generation take over.

A further challenge for us as parents is not to invest our own expectations and aspirations in our children. It stops us from perceiving them as different, and that they too might be successful but in a very different way to our generation. We should remember the song *'I did it my way'!*

And instead of discussing all of these issues openly and honestly, family members let them fester.

How should a family business plan for succession?

FBA has produced a set of 'best practice' principles for family businesses.

One important principle is the need for a Family Code of Conduct. This is a non-binding document that guides the overlap between family and business values.

The Family Code of Conduct specifies the relationship between the family and the business, and provides guidelines for resolution of issues and how the business is to be managed ongoing. It is designed to preserve harmony, promote communication and reduce conflict between family members.

In planning for succession, you also can't ignore the power behind the throne. If you want your strategy to work, involve your spouse! Also, bring your children into the discussions.

Can you give an example of a family succession plan that was effective?

One business owner had four children and ten grandchildren. Many of them worked in the business, and all of them wanted to acquire the business when he retired.

Three years before he intended to transition the business, the business owner nominated his retirement date. This gave him time to groom a successor, and also enabled him to plan a tax-effective exit.

The next thing he did was to tell all of his family members his retirement date. So, he made his plans transparent.

He said to them *'you have three years to consider what attributes the next leader of our business should have.'* The family members then all started workshopping this issue, listing out the required qualities on butchers paper in the office and discussing them in detail.

Due to the size and complexity of the business, it became apparent that the next leader really needed an MBA (Masters of Business Administration) qualification. Well, doing an MBA is a big commitment, and this caused two-thirds of the group to self-eliminate.

When the successor was finally chosen, he undertook the MBA course full time in the year before the transition.

This wise business owner then promptly extracted himself from the business when his successor took over. He moved right out of the office, allowing the successor to be his own person and run the business in his own way.

Alan Rodway

Alan is a well known business coach and executive mentor. He is the principal of Oz Business Coaching, and holds various private company directorships.

Alan has mentored the owners of some of Australia's largest family-owned businesses before, during and after their succession processes, including major IPOs and trade sales. He speaks and presents workshops regularly on this subject.

What business succession mistakes do you commonly encounter?

The first problem is that business owners don't realise that they have an ownership succession event looming – it's not front of mind. So, there is no planning and they make no changes to deal with it.

The second thing is that the awareness is there, but it is rejected. By this I mean that the emotional side of these issues is too strong and overwhelming, and can cause people to back away. Or, they don't know what to do, so tend to ignore it.

You have sometimes called this conundrum 'The Ownership Monster'. Why?

I call it a monster because it is something that lurks deep within every private business.

It is also a monster because it is an enormously confronting animal. It is multi-faceted, and consumes an awful lot of time and resources.

How can business owners overcome The Ownership Monster?

It is always different, depending on the personalities of the people involved. It is not as simple as saying *'you have an issue, so deal with it'.*

Sometimes we address it over a period of time. Sometimes we use other people to soften the blow a bit. The approach, and the time it takes to get the message through, is different in every case.

In family-owned business, what are the traps when looking to transition to the next generation?

The most obvious is appointing the next generation into positions that they do not have the skills and knowledge to handle. Even significant training and upskilling cannot get some of them to the level that an external candidate would operate at.

159

That said, the raw emotion of a father or mother saying to their son or daughter *'you are not up to this role'* is extremely difficult to deal with.

What are some of the upsides and downsides of a trade sale versus transitioning to the next generation?

To go down the trade sale route, the barrier is that the business has been successfully built based around the owner's skill set. The purchaser then looks at the business and thinks *'the very reason that this business is successful is going to walk out the door when I buy it'*. So, they discount the price, or the business won't be attractive enough to buy in the first place. I have said this in a simplistic way, but it is a real issue.

In terms of selling or gifting the business to the next generation, a series of problems cut in.

First, if there is more than one son or daughter, they invariably have different attitudes and different levels of competence to work in the business. For example, you might have one child who has worked in the business for a while and has accumulated some money to be able to buy in, but another one who hasn't. So, you need to get some sort of consistency across that generation with the support of mum and dad. That's often not easy and can take a lot of time.

If the business is gifted to the children, that comes with a downside - things which are not earned are sometimes not valued, and sometimes not understood. You have to look at each case on its merits, but my first reaction to gifting equity to the next generation is adverse. It normally doesn't work.

On the other hand, if the parents are going to sell the business at full market value to the children, then you may have a funding issue. That issue can be got around in various ways, like future dividend payments being used to fund the acquisition.

Are there any features which are common to the successful exit processes in which you have been involved?

The first thing that comes to my mind is that you need external people on the highest decision-making body of the business.

Secondly, you are talking about an *absolute stone minimum* time period of two to three years preparation if you want to do this properly. Absolute minimum. And that's really difficult because the owners can find that hard to accept, particularly if they want to leap straight into a sale.

Thirdly, you need someone with an understanding of the business, its power structures and dynamics who can gain the trust of the business owners and guide them through this process. That person needs to understand and co-ordinate the legal, tax and accounting expertise. If those expert advisers are not properly co-ordinated, the expense of running this process is horrendous and way less effective than it should be. Each of the advisers needs to be in sync with the others, and they all need to keep in regular contact.

The strongest thing I would say is that *the large majority of privately-owned businesses just don't get it.*

They think that they are across the issues, that they can just go and sell their business or give it to their kids, and that it will be easy. The reality is very different, and can be enormously difficult to confront.

So, the biggest thing that I would say to anybody is just accept the possibility – *the possibility –* that you need to go through a succession planning process and be open-minded to that.

Don't make your mind up about anything, but just accept the possibility that you need to sit down and have a really good discussion about this with someone who has working expertise in the area.

And, whilst confronting, that discussion might be the best thing you have ever done.

Your exit strategy checklist

This checklist is to be used as a starting point in planning for your exit strategy.

Please note that it is generic in nature, and is not tailored to any particular business or industry. It should not be taken as an all-encompassing document, and must be used with care.

1. Your personal position and goals

What are your medium-to-long-term personal and financial goals?

_____

_____

_____

_____

What are your current and future requirements for income?

_____

_____

_____

_____

What assets and liabilities do you have outside the business?

_____

_____

_____

_____

Is the balance between your personal and business assets appropriate?

_____

_____

_____

_____

Are your assets enough for your circumstances and to achieve your goals?

_____

_____

_____

_____

Do you have an estate plan, including wills, powers of attorney and the like?

_____

_____

_____

_____

Have you discussed business succession issues with your spouse, family or professional adviser? If so, were those discussions useful and did they play out as you had expected?

_____

_____

_____

_____

2. Succession options

Do you have a written business succession plan? If so, when was the plan last reviewed and updated?

_____

_____

_____

_____

Does your health have any bearing on your succession plans?

_____

_____

_____

_____

What is your ideal time frame for ownership succession?

_____

_____

_____

_____

How do you see your management role evolving over that period?

_____

_____

_____

_____

Is transferring your business to family members an option? If so, what roles will they take and do they require additional skills/training/experience? Has any of this been discussed with them or other family members?

_____

_____

_____

_____

Are you aware of any competitors who may be interested in acquiring the business? If so, what might be the impediments to selling your business to them?

_____

_____

_____

_____

Is your business of a sufficient size and profile to consider an IPO?

_____

_____

_____

_____

Do you have any other potential exit strategies in mind?

_____

_____

_____

_____

What are the key upsides and downsides of your potential exit strategies?

_____

_____

_____

_____

3. Preparing your business for succession

Have you conducted a review of all key aspects of the business, including:

- Historical financial information? .... Yes/No

- Key customer agreements? .... Yes/No

- Key supplier agreements? .... Yes/No

- Regulatory and legal compliance? .... Yes/No

- Real property leases/freeholds/environmental issues?............ Yes/No

- Financing arrangements? .... Yes/No

- Employment agreements with senior staff? .... Yes/No

- Stock and inventory? .... Yes/No

- Plant and equipment?... Yes/No

- Working capital management? .... Yes/No

- Taxation compliance? .... Yes/No ·

- Claims and litigation? .... Yes/No

- IT systems? .... Yes/No

- Other workflow management systems and procedures? .... Yes/No

- Human resources capability, policies, systems and procedures? . Yes/No

- SWOT analysis (strengths, weaknesses, opportunities and threats)? .. Yes/No

Have you put in place a plan to address the findings of that review? If so, what is the time frame for that plan and who within the business has the responsibility for delivering on the plan?

_____

_____

_____

_____

If not, how will you make the time and allocate appropriate resources?

_____

_____

_____

_____

If the business has more than one owner, do you have an up-to-date shareholders agreement (or similar agreement) that contains clear succession/exit mechanisms? If not, what mechanisms would be appropriate for your business?

_____

_____

_____

_____

Have you considered taking out ownership protection insurance, key person insurance, and / or income protection insurance?

_____

_____

_____

_____

Have you started preparing or mentoring your potential management successor? If not, what steps need to be taken?

_____

_____

_____

_____

Do you have a written business strategy document? Do you update this document regularly? What are the key aspects of your strategy?

_____

_____

_____

_____

Have you discussed business succession with your accountant, financial planner, lawyer or other adviser?

_____

_____

_____

_____

4. Your action points

Bearing in mind all of the above, what are your action points for:

The next week?

_____

_____

_____

_____

The next month?

_____
_____
_____
_____

The next six months?

_____
_____
_____
_____

The next year?

_____
_____
_____
_____

Useful resources

Family Business Australia — www.fambiz.org.au

Family Business Australia is the peak body for family and private business in Australia. Members include multi-generational family businesses, first generation operators, multi-sibling/cousin owned businesses and their advisers.

Financial Planning Association of Australia — www.fpa.asn.au

The Financial Planning Association of Australia is the peak industry body for financial planners in Australia. Members comprise qualified financial planners who can assist with ownership protection insurance, key person insurance, wealth creation and business succession generally.

Dynamic Small Business Network — www.dsbn.com.au

DSBN is a one-stop resource addressing the essential needs of small business. DSBN brings together articles, business tools, useful downloads, small business information, and information on events and seminars.

By Dr. Tom McKaskill — all available online at www.tommckaskill.com

- *'Invest to Exit'* – this book provides strategies for venture capital and 'business angel' investors to grow value by focussing on the endgame of exit.
- *'When potential beats profit – It is not always the balance sheet that makes a business look attractive to a would-be buyer'*. This short article looks at how finding a strategic buyer can help you to sell for a super profit. It is free to download.
- *'Investor Pitch'*. This very useful document provides guidance on how to prepare a pitch to venture capital or private equity investors. It is full of practical hints and tips, and is also free to download.

By David Maister

'Strategy and the Fat Smoker: doing what's obvious but not easy' – Spangle Press (2008)

Mills Oakley Lawyers — www.millsoakley.com.au

Mills Oakley is a medium-sized full service commercial law firm, with offices in Melbourne, Sydney and Brisbane. Mills Oakley provides legal advice to clients on all aspects of business succession.

The CEO Circle — theceocircle.com

The CEO Circle offers a confidential forum for business leaders to meet and talk honestly about issues that face them.

ASX: the Australian Securities Exchange — www.asx.com.au

The ASX website contains plenty of useful information for companies which are looking to IPO.

Index

Bonus information

I can't tell you everything that you need to know about business succession in one small book.

So, I have created a website that provides lots of additional information to assist you. Please visit www.thestrategicexit.com.

Ordering copies of this book

You may order more copies of this book in the following ways:

- Log on to www.thestrategicexit.com, which has a secure electronic payment facility.
- E-mail me on mchecketts@millsoakley.com.au

CPSIA information can be obtained at www.ICGtesting.com
Printed in the USA
BVOW021243170812

298160BV00004B/3/P

9 780980 757903